Introduction to High-Performance Blending

Culinary Techniques and Recipes for Your Vitamix Blender

VITAMIX G-SERIES

Welcome to the Next Step in Your Culinary Journey

At Vitamix, our love for healthy, delicious food runs deep within our soul. The following recipes are designed by our team of chefs to help you save time and develop unforgettable meals for family and friends.

Learn the variety of culinary techniques outlined in the Kitchen Basics section, then begin to experiment with your own creations. From simple blends to perfect emulsifications and crunchy salads to the smoothest purées, a Vitamix machine makes every meal faster, easier, and more delicious.

The recipes in this book were designed to take advantage of the incomparable versatility and power of your Vitamix machine. Its powerful performance, partnered with these delicious recipes, will help ensure your success and inspire your creativity. Explore your cookbook to find healthy, whole-food recipes, as well as a few indulgences for special occasions. We recommend starting with a simple smoothie to help you learn the functions of your new product. But don't stop there. Your Vitamix machine can create a variety of dishes for breakfast, lunch, dinner, and in-between snacks. So keep exploring. There's always a new recipe hiding in your fridge or pantry.

For more recipes and inspiration, visit **vitamix.com**.

More Than a Blender

Behind every great art, there is a careful science.

Through nearly a century of research and development, we've never stopped innovating to continually produce some of the world's best performing and most reliable blending equipment. It's our engineering story that gives professional chefs and home cooks the ability to achieve silky smooth textures and flavorful ingredient combinations.

Comprehensive Design

Vitamix takes a comprehensive approach to designing its products so that every piece works together to create a more perfect blend. We don't aim to achieve the highest horsepower. Horsepower is meaningless without a cabin and a steering wheel. Instead, we've designed a complete blending system. A motor that maintains an even torque and cool temperature at high speeds to consistently deliver the power you need to process any ingredient. A container that creates a funneling vortex to rotate ingredients through the blades. And blades that are cut, not stamped, from hardened stainless steel to pulverize ingredients and remain forceful for years to come.

Versatile Applications

Through this comprehensive approach to engineering, we've created a technology that masters a variety of techniques and recipes. From light whipped creams to heavy nut butters and hot soups to frozen desserts, Vitamix machines can be used several times a day to create entire meals, and then clean themselves.

Superior Blends

Many chefs will tell you that Vitamix virtually eliminates the need for a chinois or strainer because of the amazing textures they create. Vitamix machines make it easy to create healthy, delicious meals from natural, flavorful ingredient combinations.

Advanced Precision

With Variable Speed Control, Pulse, and Pre-Programmed Settings, Vitamix machines give home chefs complete control over speed and texture. Ingredients can be added during processing to layer course chops over smooth purées, creating hearty soups and sauces.

Greater Longevity

We don't make disposable appliances. Vitamix products are designed and built with the highest quality components that will serve you for years to come. Our customers come back to us for wedding and graduation gifts, second blenders for their vacation homes, or to buy the latest technology when they pass their old (but still functional) blenders on to their grandchildren. That's what high-performance is all about.

Getting Started

Simple tips for getting started with your new Vitamix machine

 STEP 1 CLEANING

Fill the container half-way with warm water, add a drop of dish soap, and secure the lid. Start the machine and slowly increase to its highest speed. Run for 60 seconds or use the cleaning program and rinse with warm water.

 STEP 2 INGREDIENTS

Add ingredients to the container in the order they appear in the recipe, or follow the diagram when creating your own recipes.

STEP 3 START-UP

When starting your machine, hold at a low speed (1 or 2) for a few seconds until you see the ingredients begin to circulate.

 STEP 4 SPEED

Once ingredients begin circulating, slowly rotate the dial to the speed recommended in your recipe. High speeds create a faster, smoother blend, so don't be afraid to accelerate to 10.

 STEP 5 TAMPER

The tamper presses thick and frozen mixtures into the blades to keep them circulating. While the machine is running and the lid is on, remove the lid plug and insert the tamper through the opening. Don't worry—the tamper won't touch the blades.

 STEP 6 TIME

Blend for the full processing time suggested in the recipe. Most recipes are done in less than 60 seconds, soups and sauces in less than 7 minutes.

 STEP 7 PULSE

Sometimes all you need is a quick chop of ingredients. Your machine may have a special Pulse switch to accomplish this. But if not, simply turn the machine on and off until the desired consistency is reached.

STEP 8 PROGRAMS

The recipes in this book have been written to be compatible with multiple Vitamix products. If you're working with a machine that offers pre-programmed settings, an icon at the top of the recipe will direct you to the appropriate program. Otherwise, manual processing instructions are detailed in the body of each recipe.

 Perfect for blending delicate fruits and veggies into silky smoothies

 Brings dishes to hot serving temperatures right in the blender

 Makes sorbet, ice cream, and more with the press of a button

 Blends sauce ingredients to perfectly smooth textures

 Self cleans in 60 seconds with a drop of soap and warm water

Ice & Frozen
Ingredients

Fruits & Veggies

Leafy Greens

Dry Goods (grains,
seasonings, powders)

Liquids
(water, juice, yogurt)

Note:
*If ingredients
aren't flowing, you
may need to add
a little more liquid
from the recipe,
whether it's water,
juice, broth, etc.*

Kitchen Basics

Recipes

Master a variety of culinary techniques that your Vitamix machine can achieve, from simple blends to perfect emulsifications and crunchy salads to the smoothest purées.

Kitchen Basics

PURÉE / CHOP / EMULSIFY

Blending

From nutrition-packed breakfast smoothies and whole-food juices to restaurant-style cocktails, these recipes will show you how to expertly prepare delicious beverages in your Vitamix machine.

Going Green Smoothie

Preparation: 10 minutes | **Processing:** 45 seconds
Yield: 6½ cups (1.5 l)

1 cup (240 ml) water

2 cup (300 g) green grapes

1 cup (150 g) pineapple chunks

1 ripe banana, peeled

4 cups (120 g) fresh spinach, packed

1 cup (240 ml) ice cubes

1. Place all ingredients into the Vitamix container in the order listed and firmly secure the lid.

2. Select Variable 1.

3. Start machine and slowly increase to its highest speed.

4. Blend for 45 seconds, or until desired consistency is reached.

Nutritional Information

Amount Per 1 Cup (240 ml) Serving: *Calories 70, Total Fat 0g, Saturated Fat 0g, Cholesterol 0mg, Sodium 30mg, Total Carbohydrate 17g, Dietary Fiber 2g, Sugars 12g, Protein 1g*

Chef's Note

If you're new to green smoothies, this is a great beginner recipe. Even though it's packed with fresh spinach, all you taste is delicious, fresh fruit.

Helpful Hints

Smoothies

When creating your own smoothie recipes, here are some helpful tips to keep in mind.

Adjust ingredient ratios until you find the perfect texture. Some smoothie enthusiasts prefer thick, can't-get-this-through-a-straw consistencies, while others enjoy thinner, almost juices. Play with the ratio (liquids: solids: ice) until you find your ideal blend. The lid plug lets you add ingredients while blending – so you never have to drink a smoothie that isn't just right.

The most delicious combinations blend sweet and acidic flavors, such as pineapple-mango, coconut-lime and strawberry-banana.

Color is important, since we eat with our eyes first. A green smoothie can quickly turn brown with the addition of blue or red berries. Especially for kids, consider the color combinations when you're playing with recipes.

Juicing

Instead of simply extracting juice, whole-food juice made in your Vitamix machine blends the entire ingredient, retaining all of its nutritious fiber and health benefits. Try a refreshing apple juice made from a single ingredient, or create a medley of flavors.

Apple Juice

Preparation: 10 minutes | **Processing:** 45 seconds
Yield: 2 cups (475 ml) strained

1½ pounds (680 g) apples, cored and quartered

⅔ cup (160 ml) cool water

1. Place all ingredients into the Vitamix container in the order listed and firmly secure the lid.

2. Select Variable 1.

3. Start machine and slowly increase to its highest speed, using the tamper to press the ingredients into the blades.

4. Blend for 45 seconds, or until desired consistency is reached.

5. Dampen cheesecloth or a filtration bag and squeeze out excess moisture. Place over a bowl and pour apple purée through. Twist until all juice is extracted into the bowl.

Nutritional Information

Amount Per 1 Cup (240 ml) Serving: *Calories 120, Total Fat 0g, Saturated Fat 0g, Cholesterol 0mg, Sodium 25mg, Total Carbohydrate 30g, Dietary Fiber 0g, Sugars 26g, Protein 0g*

Helpful Hints

Juices

Skins and seeds that are normally eaten along with a fruit or vegetable should be blended into juice recipes, such as apple, peach and tomato skins, or the seeds of small berries. Other skins and seeds that are normally discarded can be blended for added nutritional benefits, but may also add a bitter flavor.

For a commercial-style juice without pulp, you can strain through a Vitamix filtration bag, cheesecloth, or fine mesh strainer. To maintain the highest nutritional value, leave the juice unstrained.

If your juices have a thick, smoothie-like consistency, try adding more water to the blend to create a thinner texture.

Non-Dairy Milks

You can create fresh, homemade milk from a variety of seeds, nuts, and grains, and flavor them to taste with your favorite natural sweeteners. Perfect for cooking, baking, smoothies, or pouring over whole-grain cereal, these non-dairy milks give you complete control over flavor, texture, and ingredients.

Almond Milk

Preparation: 5 minutes plus soaking | ***Processing:*** 45 seconds
Yield: 3½ cups (840 ml)

1 cup (140 g) raw almonds, soaked overnight
in enough water to cover, drained

3 cups (720 ml) water

1. Place all ingredients into the Vitamix container in the order
listed and firmly secure the lid.

2. Select Variable 1.

3. Start machine and slowly increase to its highest speed.

4. Blend for 45 seconds, or until desired consistency is reached.

5. If you prefer pulp-free milk, place a fine mesh sieve or filtration
bag over a large bowl, and slowly pour milk into sieve.

6. Store in refrigerator. Shake well before using.

Nutritional Information

Amount Per 1 Cup (240 ml) Serving: *Calories 270, Total Fat 24g,
Saturated Fat 2g, Cholesterol 0mg, Sodium 10mg, Total Carbohydrate 10g,
Dietary Fiber 6g, Sugars 2g, Protein 10g*

Helpful Hints

Non-Dairy Milks

Soaking nuts and seeds prior
to blending creates a smoother
milk that is easier to digest.
Soak the ingredients in distilled
water for at least 4 hours, or
overnight for best results.

Non-dairy milks can be used
as a substitute to dairy milk
and cream in any recipe,
including soups, baked
goods and milkshakes.

You can sweeten non-dairy
milks to taste with a variety of
natural sweeteners, including
vanilla, honey, agave and
pitted dates.

For a commercial-style milk,
strain through a Vitamix
filtration bag, cheesecloth,
or fine mesh sieve. For the
greatest nutritional value,
leave the milk unstrained.

Whipping

Homemade *whipped cream* can be a special treat on top of a blended coffee, dessert smoothie, or slice of pie. Sprinkle with chopped dark chocolate or cookie crumbs for a presentation that's a feast for the eyes.

Whipped Cream

Preparation: 1 minute | **Processing:** 10 seconds
Yield: 2¼ cups (540 ml)

2 cups (480 ml) heavy cream

1. Place cream into the Vitamix container and firmly secure the lid.

2. Select Variable 1.

3. Start machine and slowly increase to its highest speed.

4. Blend for 10 seconds, or until desired consistency is reached, using the tamper to press the ingredient into the blades if firm peaks are preferred.

Nutritional Information

Amount Per 2 Tablespoon (30 ml) Serving: Calories 90, Total Fat 10g, Saturated Fat 6g, Cholesterol 35mg, Sodium 10mg, Total Carbohydrate 1g, Dietary Fiber 0g, Sugars 0g, Protein 1g

Helpful Hints

Whipping

Use the tamper toward the end of the recipe to press the last bit of liquid into the blades.

Do not overmix, or the cream will turn to butter.

Customize your whipped cream by adding flavorful items, such as chocolate sauce, caramel sauce, chopped nuts, spices like cinnamon and nutmeg, herbs like mint, espresso powder, or peanut butter.

Churning

Use homemade butters to add flavor to a variety of meals. You can easily customize each one with spices and seasonings that complement the dish at hand.

Butter

Preparation: 10 minutes | **Processing:** 1 minute
Yield: 6 ounces (170 g)

2 cups (480 ml) heavy whipping cream

¼ teaspoon salt, or to taste

1. Place cream into the Vitamix container and firmly secure the lid.

2. Select Variable 1.

3. Start machine and slowly increase to its highest speed.

4. Blend for 1 minute, using the tamper to press the ingredient into the blades.

5. Drain butter in a fine mesh strainer.

6. Place butter in a bowl and add salt. Work butter with a spatula to remove as much liquid as possible.

7. Store in an airtight container.

Nutritional Information

Amount Per 1 Tablespoon Serving: *Calories 100, Total Fat 11g, Saturated Fat 7g, Cholesterol 40mg, Sodium 30mg, Total Carbohydrate 1g, Dietary Fiber 0g, Sugars 0g, Protein 1g*

Helpful Hints

Churning

Prepare flavored butters ahead and freeze for later use. Place butter on a piece of wax paper and roll into a log. Place in the freezer, and cut pats of butter as needed.

Toss homemade butter with pasta or vegetables, drizzle on grilled meats and seafood, or set out for guests to spread on crusty bread. Sweeter butters are perfect for waffles or pancakes.

Customize your butter recipe by adding sweet or savory flavors, including:

Herbs: Rosemary, basil, chives, coriander, dill, sage, lemongrass, lemon thyme, lavender, vanilla

Sweeteners: Honey, molasses, maple syrup, figs, prunes, raisins, dates, dried pineapple, mango or apricot

Spices: Cinnamon, nutmeg, allspice, garam masala, garlic

Purées

Purées add beautiful presentation and fresh, exquisite flavor to your favorite meals. From fruity cocktail bases to dips, spreads, sauces, and even baby food, you'll create smooth, silky textures in seconds. Simply blend whole-food ingredients to your desired consistency.

Sweet Potato Purée

Preparation: 5 minutes plus baking | **Processing:** 20 seconds
Yield: 1½ cups (360 ml)

1 medium sweet potato, about 1 pound (450 g),
baked and peeled

½ cup (120 ml) skim milk

1 teaspoon vanilla extract

1 teaspoon ground cinnamon

1. Place all ingredients into the Vitamix container in the order listed
   and firmly secure the lid.

2. Select Variable 1.

3. Start machine and slowly increase to its highest speed.

4. Blend for 20 seconds, or until desired consistency is reached, using
   the tamper to press the ingredients into the blades.

Nutritional Information

Amount Per ¼ Cup (60 ml) Serving: *Calories 80, Total Fat 0g,
Saturated Fat 0g, Cholesterol 0mg, Sodium 50mg, Total Carbohydrate 17g,
Dietary Fiber 3g, Sugars 4g, Protein 2g*

Purées

Begin every purée recipe by
cooking all the ingredients
(including fruits, vegetables,
and meats). The easiest way to
do this is by roasting. Place the
ingredients in a single layer on
a sheet tray. Drizzle with olive
oil and sprinkle with salt and
pepper. Place in a 425°F oven
and cook until fork-tender.

Carefully add the cooked
ingredients to the container,
followed by water, stock,
or another cooking liquid.
For every 1 cup of cooked
ingredients, add ¼ cup of
liquid at a time, until you see
the desired consistency begin
to develop.

Starting at Variable 1, slowly
increase to the desired speed.
The higher the speed, the
smoother the blend. If the
ingredients are not circulating
freely, remove the lid plug and
add more liquid through the lid
plug opening. Keep the tamper
nearby to press ingredients
into the blades.

Baby Food

Preparation: 10 minutes | **Processing:** 20–30 seconds | **Yield:** 2 cups (480 ml)

Fruit	**Vegetable**	**Meat**
2 cups (about 300 g) fresh or frozen unsweetened, thawed:	2 cups (about 300 g) fresh, frozen, or canned* vegetable, cooked:	2 cups (about 280 g) boneless meat, cubed and cooked:
ripe banana, peeled	sweet potatoes, peeled	chicken
ripe peach, pitted and peeled	peas	turkey
avocado, halved, pitted, and peeled	winter squash, peeled and seeded	pork
papaya, peeled, quartered, and seeded	carrots	beef
ripe mango, peeled, halved, and pitted	green beans	veal
apple, peeled, seeded, and steamed	spinach	lamb
ripe pear, peeled, seeded, and steamed	corn	

1. Place ½ cup (120 ml) water, formula, breast milk, or cooking liquid into the Vitamix container. Add 2 cups of selected ingredients to the container and firmly secure the lid.

2. Start machine and slowly increase speed to Variable 6. Increase speed as needed, depending on ingredients used and desired consistency.

3. Blend for 20 to 30 seconds. If mixture is too thick, remove lid plug and add ¼ cup (60 ml) liquid at a time through the lid plug opening until ingredients flow freely through the blades. Secure the lid plug and continue blending until desired consistency is reached.

4. Serve immediately or freeze leftover baby food in ice cube trays.

Chef's Note: Rinse canned vegetables thoroughly before blending to reduce sodium content.

Dry Chopping

Quickly chop ingredients like garlic, carrots, nuts, and cheeses for quick and easy meal prep. Using the Pulse feature or a low variable speed, you control the texture of every chop. Combine ingredients like garlic, pepper, and celery for a healthy soup base in seconds.

Chopped Cheese

Preparation: 5 minutes | **Processing:** Pulsing

1 cup (135 g) cheese, cut into 1-inch (2 cm) cubes

1. Place cheese into the Vitamix container and firmly secure the lid.
2. Select Variable 5.
3. Pulse 10 times, or until desired consistency is reached.

Chopped Walnuts

Preparation: 5 minutes | **Processing:** Pulsing

1 cup (175 g) walnuts, toasted

1. Place walnuts into the Vitamix container and firmly secure the lid.
2. Select Variable 5.
3. Pulse 5 times. Do not overmix to avoid making walnut butter.

Chopped Fresh Herbs

Preparation: 10 minutes | **Processing:** Pulsing

2 cup (100 g) stemmed fresh chives, oregano, or parsley

1. Place herb into the Vitamix container and firmly secure the lid.
2. Select Variable 5.
3. Pulse 5 times, using the tamper to press the ingredient into the blades. Stop and scrape the sides of the container. Pulse an additional 3 times.

Helpful Hints

Dry Chopping

Process just 1 cup at a time to ensure a more even, consistent chop.

Chop different vegetables together, like spinach, peppers, and onions for a quick and easy vegetable omelette.

Remember that higher speeds achieve a finer chop. You can also Pulse (using the Pulse or On/Off switch) to create a larger dice.

Keep the tamper handy to press ingredients back into the blades.

Use the chopping technique in any recipe that calls for rough chopped vegetables or shredded cheese.

Wet Chopping

This method uses water to circulate ingredients through the blades, creating a more uniform chop. Wet chopping is ideal for preparing potatoes for hashbrowns or cabbage for slaw, but is recommended for raw fruits and vegetables only. Simply drain and discard the water, or save it for soup bases or sauces.

Chopped Cabbage

Preparation: 5 minutes | **Processing:** Pulsing

1 pound (450 g) green cabbage, cleaned and cut into ½-inch (1½ cm) wedges

1. Place cabbage into the Vitamix container. Add water until cabbage floats above the blades and firmly secure the lid.

2. Select Variable 5.

3. Pulse 4 times, or until desired consistency is reached.

4. Drain cabbage and transfer to a bowl.

Chopped Mirepoix

Preparation: 5 minutes | **Processing:** Pulsing

1 medium carrot, 3½ ounces (100 g), cut into 2-inch (5 cm) pieces

2 medium celery stalks, 3½ ounces (100 g), cut into 2-inch (5 cm) pieces

2 medium white onions, 7 ounces (200 g), peeled and quartered

4½ cups (1 l) water

1. Place all ingredients into the Vitamix container in the order listed and firmly secure the lid.

2. Select Variable 2.

3. Pulse 7 times.

4. Drain and reserve for use.

Chef's Note

Mirepoix is used as a base to add flavor to stocks, soups, and sauces.

Helpful Hints

Wet Chopping

Wet chopping is ideal for creating a perfectly uniform dice, such as chopping potatoes for hash browns or cabbage for slaw.

Place the ingredients into the container, and add just enough water to cause them to float above the blades.

After selecting the appropriate speed, quickly Pulse to the desired consistency. (If your machine does not include a Pulse feature, you can achieve the same results by quickly turning the machine on and off.) To create a larger chop, select a lower speed.

This method is only recommended for raw fruits and vegetables.

Emulsifying

Easily adjust dressings and marinades to your own flavor profiles by substituting different herbs and spices. As chefs say, "walk through the garden" to see what you have on hand.

Basic Vinaigrette

Preparation: 10 minutes | **Processing:** 25 seconds
Yield: 2 cup (480 ml)

1½ cups (360 ml) olive oil

½ cup (120 ml) red or white vinegar

2 teaspoon Dijon-style mustard

½ teaspoon ground black pepper

1 teaspoon salt

1. Place all ingredients into the Vitamix container in the order listed and firmly secure the lid.

2. Select Variable 1.

3. Start machine and slowly increase speed to Variable 7.

4. Blend for 25 seconds.

Nutritional Information

Amount Per 2 Tablespoon (30 ml) Serving: *Calories 190, Total Fat 21g, Saturated Fat 3g, Cholesterol 0mg, Sodium 135mg, Total Carbohydrate 0g, Dietary Fiber 0g, Sugars 0g, Protein 0g*

Helpful Hints

Emulsifying

When adding oil through the lid plug opening, lower the blender speed and drizzle the oil through slowly. This will give the oil enough time to fully incorporate with the rest of the ingredients, creating a perfectly smooth dressing.

Store dressings in the fridge in an airtight container (preferably glass) for up to 7 days.

Homemade dressings can be easily adjusted to suit your tastes. Fresh herbs, a blend of sweet and citrus flavors, and perhaps a bit of spice quickly awaken a bed of fresh greens.

Heating

From soups and sauces to hot beverages, blend raw ingredients and bring them to serving temperatures, right in your Vitamix container. You'll know the recipe is ready when you see steam rising from the vented lid.

Cabbage Soup

Preparation: 25 minutes | ***Processing:*** 5 minutes 45 seconds
Yield: 7½ cups (1.8 l)

2 cups (480 ml) chicken broth

2 Tablespoons (30 ml) white wine

¼ onion (35 g), chopped

½ medium carrot, 1 ounce (30 g)

10½ ounces (300 g) potato,
baked and quartered

¼ teaspoon caraway seed

1 teaspoon dried dill weed

¼ teaspoon hot sauce

½ teaspoon salt

Pinch of ground black pepper

4 cups (350 g) chopped cabbage
(See Wet Chopping)

1. Place broth, wine, onion, carrot, potato, caraway, dill weed, hot sauce, salt, and pepper into the Vitamix container in the order listed and firmly secure the lid.

2. Select Variable 1.

3. Start machine and slowly increase to its highest speed.

4. Blend for 5 minutes 45 seconds, or until heavy steam escapes from the vented lid.

5. Meanwhile, cook chopped cabbage in a large skillet with ½ cup (120 ml) to 1 cup (240 ml) water until tender.

6. Drain excess water. Place cooked cabbage into serving bowls. Pour soup over cabbage.

Nutritional Information

Amount Per 1 Cup (240 ml) Serving: *Calories 60, Total Fat 0g, Saturated Fat 0g, Cholesterol 0mg, Sodium 280mg, Total Carbohydrate 11g, Dietary Fiber 2g, Sugars 3g, Protein 2g*

Helpful Hints

Heating

The speed and power of the Vitamix blades create smooth, creamy soups from virtually any ingredient, without the need for added fat. So spare a few calories by omitting the milk or cream from your soup recipes. Or try adding a bit of avocado or a few cashews to achieve a thicker, creamy texture.

Remember that flavors of aromatic ingredients like garlic, onion, herbs and spices are intensified in the Vitamix blender, so add them in small quantities and increase gradually to taste.

You can create a delicious soup by placing any vegetable into the Vitamix container, and adding stock or cooking liquid until the liquid is about ½ inch above the ingredient. Blend on the highest speed for 5 to 6 minutes, or until heavy steam escapes from the vented lid.

Grinding

With the ability to grind whole ingredients in seconds, you can create homemade flours, seasonings, and fresh coffee grounds. The tamper helps you press dry ingredients into the blades to keep them circulating for faster processing.

Whole-Grain Flour

Preparation: 5 minutes | **Processing:** 1 minute | **Yield:** 2 cups (400 g)

2 cups (400 g) whole kernel grain

1. Place whole kernel grain into the Vitamix container and firmly secure the lid.

2. Select Variable 1.

3. Start machine and slowly increase to its highest speed.

4. Blend up to 1 minute, depending on desired fineness.

5. Store flour at room temperature for up to 1 month, or refrigerate for up to 2 months. For longer storage, flour can be frozen for 6 to 12 months. Bring flour to room temperature before use.

Cajun Spice Blend

Preparation: 10 minutes | **Processing:** 30 seconds
Yield: 1½ cups (360 ml)

4 Tablespoons (30 g) hot paprika	Pinch of cayenne
3 Tablespoons (20 g) black peppercorns	½ cup (110 g) firmly packed brown sugar
2 Tablespoons (10 g) cumin seed	1 Tablespoon whole allspice
2 Tablespoons (10 g) coriander seed	2 Tablespoons (35 g) sea salt

1. Place all ingredients into the Vitamix container and firmly secure the lid.

2. Select Variable 1.

3. Start machine and slowly increase to its highest speed.

4. Blend for 30 seconds, or until desired consistency is reached.

Grinding

Higher speeds create finer grounds, allowing you to adjust consistency with a simple rotation of the dial. Flour and coffee beans can be processed at medium speeds, but nut butters should always be processed at your blender's highest speed.

Use the tamper to press dry ingredients into the blades. Don't worry – the tamper can't touch the blades when the lid is securely in place.

For the best results, process 1 cup at a time for no longer than 1 minute.

Store freshly ground items in the fridge in airtight containers for the longest use.

If you plan to use these recipes frequently, consider purchasing a Dry Grains Container. Its blades are specially designed to efficiently process dry ingredients and mix dough. This will also protect your regular container from being scratched by whole grains.

Batters

Vitamix batters save you time and come out light and fluffy for the perfect bakes. From delicious breakfast crêpes to nutritious muffins and quick breads, fill your home with the sweet aroma of baked goods, served fresh from the oven.

Crêpe Batter

Preparation: 10 minutes | **Processing:** 1 minute
Yield: 4 cups (960 ml)

¾ cup (180 ml) plus
2½ Tablespoons (45 ml) cold water

1 cup (240 ml) cold milk

3 Tablespoons (40 g) butter, melted

4 large eggs

1½ cups (190 g) all-purpose flour

1 teaspoon salt

2 Tablespoons (30 ml) vegetable oil,
plus 1 teaspoon for cooking

1. Place water, milk, butter, eggs, flour, salt, and 2 Tablespoons (30 ml) vegetable oil into the Vitamix container in the order listed and firmly secure the lid.

2. Select Variable 1.

3. Start machine and slowly increase speed to Variable 8.

4. Blend for 25 seconds, or until desired consistency is reached.

5. Heat a 7-inch (18-cm) nonstick skillet over high heat. Add 1 teaspoon vegetable oil and heat.

6. Pour 2 Tablespoons (30 ml) crêpe batter into the skillet and swirl to cover the bottom of the pan.

7. Cook until set and remove from pan. Repeat with remaining batter. Serve with your favorite fillings, such as banana slices with hazelnut spread, strawberries with whipped cream, or spinach with feta.

Nutritional Information

Amount Per Crêpe: *Calories 50, Total Fat 2.5g, Saturated Fat 0.5g, Cholesterol 30mg, Sodium 90mg, Total Carbohydrate 6g, Dietary Fiber 0g, Sugars 1g, Protein 2g*

Helpful Hints

Batters

Add the ingredients to the container in the order in which they appear in the recipe to achieve the fastest, smoothest blends.

Process batters for the length of time recommended in the recipe. Overmixing can cause the batter to become dense.

Allow batters to rest before baking to allow the leavening agent to react.

Kneading

The Vitamix machine makes it so easy to knead thick yeast dough for breads and pizza crusts. And with the ability to grind fresh flours, you can make homemade baked goods completely from scratch.

Pizza Dough

Preparation: 15 minutes | **Processing:** 5 seconds plus Pulsing
Bake Time: 12–15 minutes | **Yield:** 1 large or 2 very thin crusts

3 lightly filled and level cups (375 g) all-purpose flour

1¾ teaspoons instant fast-rise yeast

1¼ teaspoons salt

3¾ teaspoons olive oil

11 ounces (320 ml) hot water

1. Preheat oven to 425°F (220°C). Lightly grease a large mixing bowl and set aside.

2. Place flour, yeast, and salt into the Vitamix container and firmly secure the lid.

3. Select Variable 1.

4. Start machine and slowly increase speed to Variable 8. Blend for 5 seconds. Turn machine off and remove lid plug.

5. Select Variable 3.

6. Pulse about 60 short times in 45 seconds while slowly adding oil and water through the lid plug opening until a ball forms.

7. After ball has formed, Pulse continuously for 10 to 15 seconds.

8. With floured hands, remove dough and form into a round ball. Place in prepared mixing bowl, turning over to grease on all sides. Let rise 10 minutes for a thin crust or 15 minutes for a thick crust. Stretch into pizza and top as desired. Bake for 12 to 15 minutes.

Nutritional Information

Amount per Serving (⅛ of large pizza without toppings): *Calories 190, Total Fat 2.5g, Saturated Fat 0g, Cholesterol 0mg, Sodium 360mg, Total Carbohydrates 36g, Dietary Fiber 2g, Sugars 0g, Protein 7g*

Frozen Desserts

A frozen dessert made from all-natural ingredients is the perfect way to end any meal. Use the tamper to press frozen ingredients into the blades for a smooth, even blend in seconds.

Peach Soy Sherbet

Preparation: 15 minutes | **Processing:** 1 minute
Yield: 3½ cups (840 ml)

1 cup (240 ml) soy milk

1 teaspoon vanilla extract

1 pound (450 g) frozen unsweetened peach slices

¼ cup (50 g) granulated sugar or other sweetener, to taste

1. Place all ingredients into the Vitamix container in the order listed and firmly secure the lid.

2. Select Variable 1.

3. Start machine and slowly increase to its highest speed, using the tamper to press the ingredients into the blades.

4. Blend for 1 minute, or until desired consistency is reached.

Nutritional Information

Amount Per ½ Cup (120 ml) Serving: *Calories 70, Total Fat 0.5g, Saturated Fat 0g, Cholesterol 0mg, Sodium 20mg, Total Carbohydrate 16g, Dietary Fiber 1g, Sugars 13g, Protein 2g*

Frozen Desserts

Use the tamper to quickly press frozen ingredients into the blades for the fastest, smoothest blends. There's wvno need to be delicate – the tamper can't come into contactwith the blades when the lid is firmly in place.

When creating your own frozen dessert recipe, use a simple ratio of 1 pound frozen fruit to 1 cup liquid to get the consistency just right.

Liquid ingredients can include water, juice, milk, or yogurt.

Try substituting different fruits, such as blueberries, blackberries, or a peach-mango combination.

Allowing frozen fruits to thaw at room temperature for 10 to 15 minutes before blending to help achieve a light, silky consistency.

Blend frozen desserts for about 60 seconds. You'll know the dessert is ready to serve when you stop the machine, remove the lid, and see four distinct quadrants in the container.

Beverages

From nutrition-packed breakfast smoothies and juices to restaurant-style cocktails, these recipes will show you how to expertly prepare delicious beverages in your Vitamix machine.

Beverages

SMOOTHIES / MILKS / COCKTAILS

Blackberry Pear Smoothie

Preparation: 10 minutes | **Processing:** 45 seconds | **Yield:** 5 cups (1.2 l)

¾ cup (160 ml) water

1 cup (240 g) plain yogurt

2 ripe bananas, peeled

1 ripe pear, quartered and seeded

1 medium apple, quartered and seeded

2 cups (280 g) frozen unsweetened blackberries

1. Place all ingredients into the Vitamix container in the order listed and firmly secure the lid.

2. Select Variable 1 or the Smoothie program.

3. Start machine, slowly increase to its highest speed, and blend for 45 seconds; or start machine and allow programmed cycle to complete.

Nutritional Information

Amount Per 1 Cup (240 ml) Serving: *Calories 150, Total Fat 2g, Saturated Fat 1g, Cholesterol 5mg, Sodium 25mg, Total Carbohydrate 34g, Dietary Fiber 6g, Sugars 23g, Protein 3g*

Frozen Strawberry Grape Smoothie 💧

Preparation: 10 minutes | ***Processing:*** 45 seconds | ***Yield:*** 2½ cups (600 ml)

1 cup (150 g) green grapes

1 cup (150 g) red grapes

1 cup (150 g) frozen unsweetened strawberries

½ cup (120 ml) ice cubes

1. Place all ingredients into the Vitamix container in the order listed and firmly secure the lid.

2. Select Variable 1 or the Smoothie program.

3. Start machine, slowly increase to its highest speed, and blend for 45 seconds; or start machine and allow programmed cycle to complete.

Nutritional Information

Amount Per 1 Cup (240 ml) Serving: *Calories 100, Total Fat 0g, Saturated Fat 0g, Cholesterol 0mg, Sodium 0mg, Total Carbohydrate 27g, Dietary Fiber 2g, Sugars 21g, Protein 1g*

Fruit Salad Smoothie 💧

Preparation: 20 minutes | **Processing:** 45 seconds | **Yield:** 4¾ cups (1.1 l)

½ cup (75 g) green grapes

1 medium orange, peeled, halved, and seeded

½-inch-thick (1½ cm) slice pineapple, core included, halved

½ cup (65 g) peeled and chopped cucumber

1 medium carrot, halved

1 medium apple, quartered and seeded

2½ cups (480 ml) ice cubes

1. Place all ingredients into the Vitamix container in the order listed and firmly secure the lid.

2. Select Variable 1 or the Smoothie program.

3. Start machine, slowly increase to its highest speed, and blend for 45 seconds; or start machine and allow programmed cycle to complete.

Nutritional Information

Amount Per 1 Cup (240 ml) Serving: *Calories 50, Total Fat 0g, Saturated Fat 0g, Cholesterol 0mg, Sodium 15mg, Total Carbohydrate 12g, Dietary Fiber 2g, Sugars 9g, Protein 1g*

Mixed Berry and Green Tea Smoothie ◉

Preparation: 10 minutes | **Processing:** 45 seconds | **Yield:** 5¼ cups (1.2 l)

1½ cups (360 ml) green tea, chilled

2 Tablespoons (30 ml) honey

1½ oranges, peeled and seeded

1 ripe banana, peeled, frozen, and halved

2 cups (280 g) frozen unsweetened mixed berries

1. Place all ingredients into the Vitamix container in the order listed and firmly secure the lid.

2. Select Variable 1 or the Smoothie program.

3. Start machine, slowly increase to its highest speed, and blend for 45 seconds; or start machine and allow programmed cycle to complete.

Nutritional Information

Amount Per 1 Cup (240 ml) Serving: *Calories 80, Total Fat 0g, Saturated Fat 0g, Cholesterol 0mg, Sodium 0mg, Total Carbohydrate 22g, Dietary Fiber 3g, Sugars 16g, Protein 1g*

Cucumber Melon Smoothie

Preparation: 25 minutes | ***Processing:*** 45 seconds | ***Yield:*** 3½ cups (840 ml)

¼ cup (60 ml) soy milk

1 cup (150 g) green grapes

1½ cups (240 g) cantaloupe chunks

½ cup (65 g) peeled and chopped cucumber

1 cup (170 g) honeydew chunks

½ small lime, peeled

1¼ cups (300 ml) ice cubes

1. Place all ingredients into the Vitamix container in the order listed and firmly secure the lid.

2. Select Variable 1 or the Smoothie program.

3. Start machine, slowly increase to its highest speed, and blend for 45 seconds; or start machine and allow programmed cycle to complete.

Nutritional Information

Amount Per 1 Cup (240 ml) Serving: *Calories 80, Total Fat 0.5g, Saturated Fat 0g, Cholesterol 0mg, Sodium 30mg, Total Carbohydrate 20g, Dietary Fiber 2g, Sugars 17g, Protein 2g*

Spring Green Smoothie ⬛

Preparation: 15 minutes | **Processing:** 45 seconds | **Yield:** 5 cups (1.2 l)

¼ cup (60 ml) water

1½ cups (225 g) green grapes

1 orange, peeled and halved

½ lemon, peeled and seeded

½ cucumber, cut into chunks

½ green apple, halved
and seeded

1 cup (65 g) kale, spine removed

1 cup (50 g) romaine lettuce

1 cup (60 g) parsley leaves

1 cup (150 g) frozen unsweetened
pineapple chunks

2 cups (480 ml) ice cubes

1. Place all ingredients into the Vitamix container in the order listed and firmly secure the lid.

2. Select Variable 1 or the Smoothie program.

3. Start machine, slowly increase to its highest speed, and blend for 45 seconds; or start machine and allow programmed cycle to complete.

Nutritional Information

Amount Per 1 Cup (240 ml) Serving: *Calories 90, Total Fat 0g, Saturated Fat 0g, Cholesterol 0mg, Sodium 15mg, Total Carbohydrate 23g, Dietary Fiber 3g, Sugars 13g, Protein 2g*

Blueberry Pineapple Smoothie ⬤

Preparation: 15 minutes | **Processing:** 45 seconds | **Yield:** 3 cups (720 ml)

¼ cup (60 ml) orange juice

¼ cup (60 ml) pineapple juice

½ cup (120 g) low-fat vanilla yogurt

1 ripe banana, peeled

2 cups (60 g) fresh spinach leaves, lightly packed

1 cup (140 g) frozen unsweetened blueberries

¼ cup (35 g) frozen dark sweet cherries

½ cup (120 ml) ice cubes

1. Place all ingredients into the Vitamix container in the order listed and firmly secure the lid.

2. Select Variable 1 or the Smoothie program.

3. Start machine, slowly increase to its highest speed, and blend for 45 seconds; or start machine and allow programmed cycle to complete.

Nutritional Information

Amount Per 1 Cup (240 ml) Serving: *Calories 130, Total Fat 1g, Saturated Fat 0g, Cholesterol 0mg, Sodium 60mg, Total Carbohydrate 29g, Dietary Fiber 4g, Sugars 20g, Protein 3g*

Minty Green Smoothie

Preparation: 10 minutes | **Processing:** 45 seconds | **Yield:** 5 cups (1.2 l)

1 cup (240 ml) water

4 cups (120 g) fresh spinach leaves

4 small mint leaves

2½ cups (375 g) fresh pineapple chunks

1½ cups (360 ml) ice cubes

1. Place all ingredients into the Vitamix container in the order listed and firmly secure the lid.

2. Select Variable 1 or the Smoothie program.

3. Start machine, slowly increase to its highest speed, and blend for 45 seconds; or start machine and allow programmed cycle to complete.

Nutritional Information

Amount Per 1 Cup (240 ml) Serving: *Calories 45, Total Fat 0g, Saturated Fat 0g, Cholesterol 0mg, Sodium 40mg, Total Carbohydrate 12g, Dietary Fiber 1g, Sugars 7g, Protein 1g*

Orange Flax Smoothie ⬤

Preparation: 15 minutes | **Processing:** 45 seconds | **Yield:** 2¾ cups (660 ml)

1 cup (240 ml) carrot juice

½ cup (120 ml) orange juice

2 Tablespoons (15 g) ground flaxseed

1 teaspoon chopped fresh ginger root

2 cups (280 g) frozen unsweetened peach slices

1. Place all ingredients into the Vitamix container in the order listed and firmly secure the lid.

2. Select Variable 1 or the Smoothie program.

3. Start machine, slowly increase to its highest speed, and blend for 45 seconds; or start machine and allow programmed cycle to complete.

Nutritional Information

Amount Per 1 Cup (240 ml) Serving: *Calories 110, Total Fat 1.5g, Saturated Fat 0g, Cholesterol 0mg, Sodium 20mg, Total Carbohydrate 23g, Dietary Fiber 4g, Sugars 16g, Protein 3g*

Carrot Cider with Ginger ⬤

Preparation: 10 minutes | *Processing:* 45 seconds | *Yield:* 3 cups (720 ml)

2 cups (480 ml) apple cider or apple juice

3 medium carrots, 6 ounces (170 g)

½ teaspoon chopped fresh ginger root

1 cup (240 ml) ice cubes

1. Place all ingredients into the Vitamix container in the order listed and firmly secure the lid.

2. Select Variable 1 or the Smoothie program.

3. Start machine, slowly increase to its highest speed, and blend for 45 seconds; or start machine and allow programmed cycle to complete.

Nutritional Information

Amount Per 1 Cup (240 ml) Serving: Calories 100, Total Fat 0g, Saturated Fat 0g, Cholesterol 0mg, Sodium 55mg, Total Carbohydrate 25g, Dietary Fiber 2g, Sugars 20g, Protein 1g

Fresh Lemonade ⬤

Preparation: 10 minutes | *Processing:* 45 seconds | *Yield:* 3 cups (720 ml)

2 cups (480 ml) water

1 lemon, peeled with 1-inch (2½ cm)
strip of peel remaining

2 Tablespoons (30 ml) honey

1 cup (240 ml) ice cubes

1. Place all ingredients into the Vitamix container in the order listed and firmly secure the lid.

2. Select Variable 1 or the Smoothie program.

3. Start machine, slowly increase to its highest speed, and blend for 45 seconds; or start machine and allow programmed cycle to complete.

Nutritional Information

Amount Per 1 Cup (240 ml) Serving: Calories 50, Total Fat 0g, Saturated Fat 0g, Cholesterol 0mg, Sodium 10mg, Total Carbohydrate 13g, Dietary Fiber 1g, Sugars 11g, Protein 0g

Lemonade Blush ◉

Preparation: 10 minutes | **Processing:** 45 seconds | **Yield:** 6 cups (1.4 l)

¼ cup agave

1 teaspoon chopped fresh rosemary

½ cup (120 ml) lemon juice

6 cups (930 g) cubed
and seeded watermelon

2–4 cups (480–960 ml) ice cubes

1. Place all ingredients into the Vitamix container in the order listed and firmly secure the lid.

2. Select Variable 1 or the Smoothie program.

3. Start machine, slowly increase to its highest speed, and blend for 45 seconds; or start machine and allow programmed cycle to complete.

Nutritional Information

Amount Per 1 Cup (240 ml) Serving: *Calories 80, Total Fat 0g, Saturated Fat 0g, Cholesterol 0mg, Sodium 5mg, Total Carbohydrate 26g, Dietary Fiber 1g, Sugars 24g, Protein 1g*

Strawberry Agua Fresca ◉

Preparation: 20 minutes | **Processing:** 45 seconds | **Yield:** 5¼ cups (1.2 l)

2 cups (300 g) fresh strawberries

4 cups (620 g) cubed
and seeded watermelon

2 Tablespoons (30 ml) lemon juice

2 cups (480 ml) ice cubes

1. Place all ingredients into the Vitamix container in the order listed and firmly secure the lid.

2. Select Variable 1 or the Smoothie program.

3. Start machine, slowly increase to its highest speed, and blend for 45 seconds; or start machine and allow programmed cycle to complete.

Nutritional Information

Amount Per 1 Cup (240 ml) Serving: Calories 25, Total Fat 0g, Saturated Fat 0g, Cholesterol 0mg, Sodium 0mg, Total Carbohydrate 7g, Dietary Fiber 2g, Sugars 6g, Protein 0g

Soy Milk

Preparation: 30 minutes plus soaking | ***Processing:*** 45 seconds | ***Yield:*** 4½ cups (1.0 l)

1 cup (200 g) dried soy beans

1 Tablespoon sugar

3½ cups (840 ml) water

1. Clean dried soy beans and soak in water for 4 to 8 hours. Steam for about 15 minutes. Drain soy beans and let cool.

2. Place 1½ cups (260 g) cooked beans, sugar, and water into the Vitamix container in the order listed and firmly secure the lid.

3. Select Variable 1 or the Smoothie program.

4. Start machine, slowly increase to its highest speed, and blend for 45 seconds; or start machine and allow programmed cycle to complete.

5. To obtain commercial-style soy milk, strain the milk through a filtration bag or pass through a fine-mesh sieve.

Nutritional Information

Amount Per 1 Cup (240 ml) Serving: *Calories 110, Total Fat 5g, Saturated Fat 0.5g, Cholesterol 0mg, Sodium 10mg, Total Carbohydrate 8g, Dietary Fiber 3g, Sugars 5g, Protein 10g*

Rice Milk

Preparation: 10 minutes plus cook time | **Processing:** 2 minutes 30 seconds
Yield: 2½ cups (600 ml)

2 cups (480 ml) water

½ cup (100 g) cooked brown rice, cooled

½ Tablespoon firmly packed brown sugar
or other sweetener, or to taste

1. Place all ingredients into the Vitamix container in the order listed
   and firmly secure the lid.

2. Select Variable 1.

3. Start machine and slowly increase to its highest speed.

4. Blend for 2 minutes 30 seconds, or until desired consistency is reached.
   Store in refrigerator. Shake well before using.

Nutritional Information

Amount Per 1 Cup (240 ml) Serving: *Calories 50, Total Fat 0g, Saturated Fat 0g,
Cholesterol 0mg, Sodium 10mg, Total Carbohydrate 12g, Dietary Fiber 1g,
Sugars 3g, Protein 1g*

Mexican Coffee

Preparation: 10 minutes | **Processing:** 15 seconds | **Yield:** 6 cups (1.4 l)

2 cinnamon sticks

4 whole cloves

6 Tablespoons (90 g) ground coffee

2 ounces (55 g) bittersweet chocolate,
coarsely chopped

Whipped Cream (See recipe in Kitchen Basics)

6 cinnamon sticks

1. Stir together cinnamon sticks, cloves, and coffee grounds.

2. Place mixture into your coffee maker according to manufacturer's instructions and brew the coffee using 6 cups (1.4 l) water.

3. Place coffee and chocolate into the Vitamix container in the order listed and firmly secure the lid.

4. Select Variable 1.

5. Start machine and slowly increase to its highest speed.

6. Blend for 15 seconds, or until chocolate is melted.

7. Divide blended coffee into six mugs. Top each serving with whipped cream and garnish with a cinnamon stick.

Nutritional Information

Amount Per 1 Cup (240 ml) Serving (with 1 Tablespoon Whipped Cream):
*Calories 160, Total Fat 15g, Saturated Fat 9g, Cholesterol 40mg, Sodium 20mg,
Total Carbohydrate 7g, Dietary Fiber 1g, Sugars 4g, Protein 1g*

Mocha Spiced Hot Cocoa

Preparation: 10 minutes | *Processing:* 5 minutes | *Yield:* 2 cups (480 ml)

1½ cups (360 ml) milk

½ cup (90 g) semisweet chocolate chips

¼ teaspoon ground cinnamon

2 teaspoons instant coffee granules

⅛ teaspoon chili powder

1. Place all ingredients into the Vitamix container in the order listed and firmly secure the lid.

2. Select Variable 1.

3. Start machine and slowly increase to its highest speed.

4. Blend for 5 minutes.

Nutritional Information

Amount Per 1 Cup (240 ml) Serving: Calories 400, Total Fat 22g, Saturated Fat 13g, Cholesterol 20mg, Sodium 80mg, Total Carbohydrate 46g, Dietary Fiber 3g, Sugars 41g, Protein 10g

Frozen Bloody Mary

Preparation: 10 minutes plus 5 hours freeze time | **Processing:** Pulsing
Yield: 6 cups (1.4 l)

3 cups (720 ml) tomato juice

1 cup (240 ml) beef broth

1 Tablespoon fresh lemon juice

1 teaspoon Worcestershire sauce

Few drops of hot sauce

½ cup (120 ml) vodka

1. Combine tomato juice, beef broth, lemon juice, Worcestershire sauce, and hot sauce in a mixing bowl. Pour into ice cube trays. Cover and freeze for 5 hours.

2. Place cubes into the Vitamix container, add vodka, and firmly secure the lid.

3. Select Variable 3.

4. Pulse a few times, or until slushy.

Nutritional Information

Amount Per 1 Cup (240 ml) Serving: *Calories 80, Total Fat 0g, Saturated Fat 0g, Cholesterol 0mg, Sodium 490mg, Total Carbohydrate 6g, Dietary Fiber 1g, Sugars 4g, Protein 2g*

Cranberry Lime Sparkle

Preparation: 10 minutes | *Processing:* 15–20 seconds | *Yield:* 3 cups (720 ml)

½ cup (120 ml) 100% cranberry juice

4 ounces (120 ml) light rum

2 ounces (60 ml) vodka

2 Tablespoons (25 g) granulated sugar

¼ small lime, peeled and seeded

¼ cup (25 g) fresh cranberries

2 cups (480 ml) ice cubes

1. Place all ingredients into the Vitamix container in the order listed and firmly secure the lid.

2. Select Variable 1.

3. Start machine and slowly increase to its highest speed.

4. Blend for 15 to 20 seconds, or until desired consistency is reached.

5. Pour into a sugar-rimmed glass and serve immediately.

Nutritional Information

Amount Per 1 Cup (240 ml) Serving: Calories 190, Total Fat 0g, Saturated Fat 0g, Cholesterol 0mg, Sodium 5mg, Total Carbohydrate 14g, Dietary Fiber 1g, Sugars 13g, Protein 0g

Strawberry Daiquiri 💧

Preparation: 10 minutes | **Processing:** 45 seconds | **Yield:** 3 cups (720 ml)

4 ounces (120 ml) light rum

2 ounces (60 ml) triple sec

2 Tablespoons (30 ml) fresh lime juice

1 cup (150 g) frozen unsweetened strawberries, softened for 10 minutes

2–4 Tablespoons (16–30 g) powdered sugar

2 cups (480 ml) ice cubes

1. Place all ingredients into the Vitamix container in the order listed and firmly secure the lid.

2. Select Variable 1 or the Smoothie program.

3. Start machine, slowly increase to its highest speed, and blend for 45 seconds; or start machine and allow programmed cycle to complete.

Nutritional Information

Amount Per 1 Cup (240 ml) Serving: *Calories 190, Total Fat 0g, Saturated Fat 0g, Cholesterol 0mg, Sodium 0mg, Total Carbohydrate 18g, Dietary Fiber 1g, Sugars 14g, Protein 0g*

Whole Fruit Margarita

Preparation: 15 minutes | **Processing:** 55 seconds | **Yield:** 6 cups (1.4 l)

¼ cup (60 ml) water

6 ounces (180 ml) tequila

2 ounces (60 ml) Grand Marnier or triple sec

1 medium orange, peeled, seeded, and halved

1 lime, peeled

1 lemon, peeled, seeded, and halved

6 Tablespoons (75 g) granulated sugar

6 cups (1.4 l) ice cubes

1. Place all ingredients into the Vitamix container in the order listed and firmly secure the lid.

2. Select Variable 1 or the Frozen Dessert program.

3. Start machine, slowly increase to its highest speed, and blend for 55 seconds; or start machine and allow programmed cycle to complete.

4. Pour into salt-rimmed margarita glasses and serve immediately.

Nutritional Information

Amount Per 1 Cup (240 ml) Serving: *Calories 150, Total Fat 0g, Saturated Fat 0g, Cholesterol 0mg, Sodium 5mg, Total Carbohydrate 20g, Dietary Fiber 1g, Sugars 18g, Protein 0g*

Planning Ahead

Made-to-Order Margaritas

This homemade margarita is made healthier and brighter-tasting with a trio of fresh citrus fruits.

Made-to-order margaritas for a group usually mean that the host has to play bartender for most of the party, but you can cut down on your prep (and join in on the fun) by peeling and seeding oranges, lemons, and limes for multiple batches beforehand. Keep the fruits in the fridge in a covered container until ready to use, and you'll be able to quickly blend them together in seconds and ensure that each drink is served icy-cold.

Mix things up by experimenting with different types of fruit, like juicy, bright orange satsumas and tangerines, sweet, pale pink naval oranges, and tangy, ruby-red blood oranges.

Piña Colada ⬛

Preparation: 20 minutes | **Processing:** 45 seconds | **Yield:** 3½ cups (840 ml)

4½ ounces (70 ml) light rum

4½ Tablespoons (70 ml)
cream of coconut

½ cup (120 ml) coconut milk

2 Tablespoons (10 g) shredded coconut

¾ cup (100 g) fresh pineapple chunks,
core included

3 cups (720 ml) ice cubes

1. Place all ingredients into the Vitamix container in the order listed
   and firmly secure the lid.

2. Select Variable 1 or the Smoothie program.

3. Start machine, slowly increase to its highest speed, and blend for 45 seconds;
   or start machine and allow programmed cycle to complete.

Nutritional Information

Amount Per 1 Cup (240 ml) Serving: Calories 230, Total Fat 7g, Saturated Fat 7g,
Cholesterol 0mg, Sodium 25mg, Total Carbohydrate 19g, Dietary Fiber 0g,
Sugars 17g, Protein 1g

Mango Margarita ❄

Preparation: 10 minutes | ***Processing:*** 55 seconds | ***Yield:*** 6 cups (1.4 l)

¼ cup (60 ml) water

¾ cup (180 ml) tequila

¼ cup (60 ml) Grand Marnier

1 orange, peeled, seeded, and halved

1 lime, peeled, seeded, and halved

2½ cups (300 g) frozen mango chunks,
partially thawed

⅓ cup (80 g) caster sugar

4 cups (960 ml) ice cubes

1. Place all ingredients into the Vitamix container in the order listed
and firmly secure the lid.

2. Select Variable 1 or the Frozen Dessert program.

3. Start machine, slowly increase to its highest speed, and blend for 55 seconds;
or start machine and allow programmed cycle to complete.

Nutritional Information

Amount Per 1 Cup (240 ml) Serving: *Calories 200, Total Fat 0g, Saturated Fat 0g,
Cholesterol 0mg, Sodium 0mg, Total Carbohydrate 31g, Dietary Fiber 3g,
Sugars 28g, Protein 1g*

Soups

Soups are a healthy and easy meal for lunch or dinner. Transform fresh vegetables into a rustic Tortilla Soup or steamy purées like Cream of Asparagus Soup.

Soups

LUNCH / DINNER

French Onion Soup ♨

Preparation: 15 minutes | **Processing:** 5 minutes 45 seconds
Cook Time: 15 minutes | **Yield:** 3½ cups (840 ml)

3 Tablespoons (45 ml)
extra virgin olive oil

4 cups (560 g) onions, sliced

2 garlic cloves, peeled
and cut into 4 slices

1 teaspoon Kosher salt

½ teaspoon granulated sugar

¼ teaspoon dried thyme leaves

⅛ teaspoon ground
black pepper

2 cups (480 ml) beef broth

¼ cup (60 ml) dry white wine

6 slices baguette bread

3 slices Swiss cheese

1. In a large nonstick skillet, heat olive oil over medium heat. Add onions and cook, partially covered, stirring occasionally, until onions soften, about 10 to 12 minutes.

2. Add garlic, salt, sugar, thyme, and pepper to the skillet. Continue cooking, stirring occasionally, until garlic softens, about 4 to 5 minutes.

3. Place onion mixture, beef broth, and wine into the Vitamix container in the order listed and firmly secure the lid.

4. Select Variable 1 or the Hot Soup program.

5. Start machine, slowly increase to its highest speed, and blend for 5 minutes 45 seconds; or start machine and allow programmed cycle to complete.

6. Pour servings of soup into oven- or broiler-safe bowls.

7. Top each serving with two baguette slices and one slice of cheese. Place under hot broiler for 45 to 60 seconds, or until cheese is melted. Serve immediately.

Nutritional Information

Amount Per 1 Cup (240 ml) Serving: *Calories 440, Total Fat 18g, Saturated Fat 5g, Cholesterol 15mg, Sodium 1320mg, Total Carbohydrate 51g, Dietary Fiber 5g, Sugars 8g, Protein 17g*

Gazpacho

Preparation: 15 minutes | *Processing:* 15 seconds | *Yield:* 8 cups (1.9 l)

3 cups (720 ml) tomato juice, fresh or canned

⅓ cup (80 ml) red wine vinegar

1 pound (455 g) ripe tomatoes (4–5 large), quartered

2½ cups (330 g) peeled and rough chopped cucumber

¼ cup (60 ml) olive oil

1 small onion (55 g), chopped

1 medium sweet green bell pepper (225 g), seeded and quartered

Dash of hot sauce

Salt, to taste

Ground black pepper, to taste

1. Place all ingredients into the Vitamix container in the order listed and firmly secure the lid.

2. Select Variable 1.

3. Start machine and slowly increase speed to Variable 2.

4. Blend for 15 seconds.

5. Season to taste with salt and pepper and serve immediately or refrigerate.

Nutritional Information

Amount Per 1 Cup (240 ml) Serving: Calories 110, Total Fat 7g, Saturated Fat 1g, Cholesterol 0mg, Sodium 340mg, Total Carbohydrate 9g, Dietary Fiber 2g, Sugars 6g, Protein 2g

Tomato Thyme Soup

Preparation: 20 minutes | **Processing:** 6 minutes
Yield: 5½ cups (1.3 l) (5 servings)

1½ cups (360 ml) water

1 (14½-ounce/410-g)
can diced tomatoes

2 Roma tomatoes, halved

1 medium carrot, halved

¾ cup (75 g) oil-packed sun
dried tomatoes, drained

1 teaspoon flaxseed

1½ Tablespoons chopped onion

1 garlic clove, peeled

½ Tablespoon fresh thyme
sprigs (leaves only if sprigs
are woody and thick)

1 teaspoon fresh oregano leaves

1 Tablespoon tomato paste

½ vegetable bouillon cube

½ cup (120 ml) whole milk,
room temperature

1. Place water, canned tomatoes, fresh tomatoes, carrot, sun dried tomatoes, flaxseed, onion, garlic, thyme, oregano, tomato paste, and bouillon into the Vitamix container in the order listed and firmly secure the lid.

2. Select Variable 1 or the Hot Soup program.

3. Start machine, slowly increase to its highest speed, and blend for 5 minutes 45 seconds; or start machine and allow programmed cycle to complete.

4. Select Variable 2.

5. Start machine and remove lid plug. Slowly add milk through the lid plug opening. Secure lid plug.

6. Slowly increase to highest speed and blend an additional 15 seconds.

Nutritional Information

Amount Per Serving: Calories 90, Total Fat 3.5g, Saturated Fat 1g, Cholesterol 5mg, Sodium 450mg, Total Carbohydrate 13g, Dietary Fiber 3g, Sugars 6g, Protein 3g

Cream of Asparagus Soup

Preparation: 10 minutes | **Processing:** 5 minutes 55 seconds
Yield: 6 cups (1.2 l)

1½ pounds (680 g) asparagus spears, cooked
(reserve 1 cup (180 g) pieces for garnish)

1½ cups (360 ml) chicken broth

⅛ teaspoon salt

⅛ teaspoon ground black pepper

½ cup (120 ml) heavy cream

1. Place asparagus, broth, salt, and pepper into the Vitamix container in
    the order listed and firmly secure the lid.

2. Select Variable 1 or the Hot Soup program.

3. Start machine, slowly increase to its highest speed, and blend for 5 minutes 45 seconds;
    or start machine and allow programmed cycle to complete.

4. Select Variable 1 and start machine. Remove the lid plug and pour heavy cream
    through the lid plug opening. Secure lid plug.

5. Slowly increase speed to Variable 8 and blend an additional 10 seconds.
    Serve immediately over reserved asparagus pieces.

Nutritional Information

Amount Per 1 Cup (240 ml) Serving: *Calories 90, Total Fat 8g, Saturated Fat 5g,
Cholesterol 30mg, Sodium 500mg, Total Carbohydrate 3g, Dietary Fiber 2g,
Sugars 1g, Protein 5g*

Chef's Note

To cook asparagus, *steam
for about 10 minutes, or
until tender. Let cool 10
minutes before blending.*

Bacon Cheddar Potato Soup

Preparation: 20 minutes | ***Processing:*** 5 minutes 55 seconds | ***Yield:*** 4 cups (960 ml)

2 cups (480 ml) milk

2 medium Russet potatoes (340 g),
baked, halved, divided use

⅔ cup (80 g) shredded
Cheddar cheese, divided use

2 Tablespoons (20 g)
chopped onion, sautéed

½ teaspoon dried dill weed

½ teaspoon salt

1 ounce (30 g) bacon, cooked

1. Place milk, one potato, half of the cheese, onion, dill, and salt into the Vitamix container in the order listed and firmly secure the lid.

2. Select Variable 1 or the Hot Soup program.

3. Start machine, slowly increase to its highest speed, and blend for 5 minutes 45 seconds; or start machine and allow programmed cycle to complete.

4. Select Variable 1.

5. Start machine and remove the lid plug. Add remaining potato, bacon, and cheese through the lid plug opening.

6. Secure lid plug and blend an additional 10 seconds.

Nutritional Information

Amount Per 1 Cup (240 ml) Serving: *Calories 260, Total Fat 13g, Saturated Fat 7g, Cholesterol 40mg, Sodium 590mg, Total Carbohydrate 22g, Dietary Fiber 1g, Sugars 7g, Protein 13g*

Tortilla Soup ♨

Preparation: 15 minutes | *Processing:* 5 minutes 55 seconds | *Yield:* 4 cups (960 ml)

Soup Base:

1 cup (240 ml) low-sodium chicken, beef, or vegetable broth

1 Roma tomato, halved

1 carrot, halved

1 celery stalk, halved

1 thin slice of onion, peeled

1 garlic clove, peeled

1 thin slice of yellow squash

1 thin slice of red bell pepper

1 thin slice of cabbage

1 mushroom

Salt, to taste

Ground black pepper, to taste

1 teaspoon taco seasoning

Dash of ground cumin

Optional Ingredients:

½ cup (70 g) cooked chicken breast

½ fresh jalapeño

¼ cup (30 g) pitted olives

¼ cup (50 g) unsalted canned corn, drained

2 ounces (60 g) baked tortilla chips

1. Place all soup base ingredients into the Vitamix container in the order listed and firmly secure the lid.

2. Place all ingredients into the Vitamix container in the order listed and firmly secure the lid.

3. Select Variable 1 or the Hot Soup program.

4. Start machine, slowly increase to its highest speed, and blend for 5 minutes 45 seconds; or start machine and allow programmed cycle to complete.

5. If adding optional ingredients, select Variable 2. Start machine and remove the lid plug. Add chicken, jalapeños, olives, corn, and chips through the lid plug opening.

6. Blend an additional 10 seconds.

Nutritional Information

Amount Per 1 Cup (240 ml) Serving: Calories 170, Total Fat 9g, Saturated Fat 1.5g, Cholesterol 10mg, Sodium 480mg, Total Carbohydrate 18g, Dietary Fiber 3g, Sugars 4g, Protein 5g

Broccoli Cheese Soup ♨

Preparation: 15 minutes | **Processing:** 5 minutes 45 seconds
Yield: 2¼ cups (540 ml) (2 servings)

1 cup (240 ml) milk

½ cup (55 g) shredded Cheddar cheese

2 cups (310 g) steamed broccoli, divided use

1 teaspoon diced onion

½ chicken bouillon cube

1. Place milk, cheese, 1½ cups broccoli, onion, and bouillon into the Vitamix container in the order listed and firmly secure the lid.

2. Select Variable 1 or the Hot Soup program.

3. Start machine, slowly increase to its highest speed, and blend for 5 minutes 45 seconds; or start machine and allow programmed cycle to complete.

4. Divide remaining ½ cup (80 g) broccoli between two serving bowls. Pour soup over broccoli and serve.

Nutritional Information

Amount Per Serving: Calories 210, Total Fat 10g, Saturated Fat 6g, Cholesterol 30mg, Sodium 530mg, Total Carbohydrate 18g, Dietary Fiber 5g, Sugars 9g, Protein 15g

Chef's Note

A healthy way to thicken this soup is to add ¼ cup canned cannelini beans, rinsed and drained, in Step 1.

Leafy Green Soup

Preparation: 20 minutes | **Processing:** 40 – 60 seconds
Cook Time: 1 hour | **Yield:** 11 cups (2.6 l)

2 Tablespoons (30 ml)
extra virgin olive oil

½ medium yellow onion (255 g),
rough chopped

1 teaspoon salt, divided use

¼ cup (50 g) uncooked Arborio rice

1 bunch, 1 pound (455 g) green chard,
white ribs removed, rough chopped

14 cups (420 g) gently packed
spinach leaves, rough chopped

4 cups (960 ml) low-sodium
vegetable broth

Large pinch of cayenne pepper

1 Tablespoon lemon juice

1. Heat oil in a large skillet over high heat. Add onions and ¼ teaspoon salt; cook, stirring frequently until the onions begin to brown, about 5 minutes. Reduce heat to low. Add 2 Tablespoons (30 ml) water and cover. Cook, stirring frequently until the pan cools. Continue stirring occasionally, always covering the pan, until the onions reduce and have a deep caramel color, about 25 to 30 minutes.

2. Combine 3 cups (720 ml) water and ¾ teaspoon salt in a Dutch oven. Add rice and bring to a boil. Reduce heat; cover and simmer for 15 minutes. Stir in chard. Return to a simmer, cover and cook for 10 minutes. Add cooked onions, spinach, broth, and cayenne. Return to a simmer. Cover and cook, stirring once until spinach is tender, about 5 minutes.

3. Place half the mixture into the Vitamix container and firmly secure the lid.

4. Select Variable 1.

5. Start machine and slowly increase speed to Variable 10.

6. Blend for 20 to 30 seconds until desired consistency is reached. Transfer to a clean soup pot and repeat blending with remaining mixture. Warm blended soup over medium heat. Stir in 1 Tablespoon lemon juice prior to serving.

Nutritional Information

Amount Per Serving: *Calories 100, Total Fat 3g, Saturated Fat 0g, Cholesterol 0mg, Sodium 500mg, Total Carbohydrates 15g, Dietary Fiber 4g, Sugars 2g, Protein 3g*

Winter Squash Soup

Preparation: 30 minutes | ***Processing:*** 35–40 seconds
Cook Time: 20–25 minutes | ***Yield:*** 6¼ cups (1.5 l) (6 servings)

1 Tablespoon olive oil

1 medium onion,
4½ ounces (130 g), chopped

2 garlic cloves, peeled and halved

2 teaspoons smoked paprika

1 bay leaf

2 Tablespoons (30 ml) dry sherry

1½ pounds (680 g) winter squash,
peeled, seeded, and cut into
1-inch (2.5 cm) pieces

2 cups (480 ml) low-sodium
vegetable broth

1 cup (240 ml) water

Sea salt, to taste

1. Heat oil in a large pot over medium-high heat. Add onion and sauté for 3 to 5 minutes. Stir in garlic, smoked paprika, and bay leaf. Cook for 1 minute.

2. Add sherry and cook for 2 minutes. Add squash, broth, and water. Bring to a simmer, cover, and reduce heat to medium-low. Cook for 20 minutes, or until squash is tender. Remove bay leaf.

3. Carefully place hot mixture into the Vitamix container and firmly secure the lid.

4. Select Variable 1.

5. Start machine and slowly increase speed to Variable 10.

6. Blend for 35 to 40 seconds.

7. Season to taste with sea salt, if desired.

Nutritional Information

Amount Per Serving: *Calories 80, Total Fat 2.5g, Saturated Fat 0g, Cholesterol 0mg, Sodium 55mg, Total Carbohydrate 13g, Dietary Fiber 3g, Sugars 4g, Protein 1g*

Sweet Potato Sage Soup

Preparation: 35 minutes | **Processing:** 1 minute 15 seconds
Cook Time: 1 hour | **Yield:** 11½ cups (2.8 l) (11 servings)

3 Tablespoons (45 ml)
extra virgin olive oil, divided use

1 cup (160 g) diced onion

1 teaspoon salt, divided use

4 garlic cloves, peeled and halved

1 teaspoon chopped fresh thyme leaves

1 large bunch kale, tough stems
removed, rough chopped

1 pound (455 g) sweet potatoes, peeled
and cut into 1-inch (2.5 cm) cubes

8 fresh sage leaves

12 ounces (340 g) fresh spinach

4 cups (960 ml) low-sodium
vegetable broth

Pinch of cayenne pepper

Pinch of ground black pepper

1 Tablespoon fresh lemon juice

1 Tablespoon honey

1. Heat 2 Tablespoons (30 ml) oil in a skillet over high heat. Add onion and ¼ teaspoon salt. Cook, stirring frequently, until the onions begin to brown, about 5 minutes. Reduce heat to low. Stir in 2 Tablespoons (30 ml) water, garlic, and thyme. Cover and cook, stirring frequently until the pan cools. Continue stirring occasionally, always covering the pan, until the onions reduce and have a deep caramel color, about 25 to 30 minutes.

2. Meanwhile, combine 4 cups (960 ml) water and ¾ teaspoon salt in a Dutch oven. Add kale, sweet potato, and sage. Bring to a boil. Reduce heat to maintain a simmer; cover and simmer for 15 minutes.

3. Stir in spinach and return to a simmer. Cover and cook for 10 minutes. When the onions are caramelized, stir a little simmering liquid into them. Scrape the bottom of the skillet to incorporate any browned bits, and transfer onion mixture to the soup. Add vegetable broth and return to a simmer. Continue cooking for 5 minutes.

4. Place half of the mixture into the Vitamix container and firmly secure the lid.

5. Select Variable 1.

6. Start machine and slowly increase speed to Variable 8.

7. Blend for 35 to 40 seconds. Transfer to a clean soup pot and repeat with remaining half. Stir in cayenne, ground black pepper, lemon juice, and honey.

Nutritional Information

Amount Per Serving: Calories 110, Total Fat 4.5g, Saturated Fat 0.5g, Cholesterol 0mg, Sodium 320mg, Total Carbohydrate 17g, Dietary Fiber 3g, Sugars 4g, Protein 3g

Leek, Artichoke & Potato Soup

Preparation: 20 minutes | **Processing:** 30–40 seconds
Cook Time: 35–40 minutes | **Yield:** 7½ cups (1.8 l) (7 servings)

2 Tablespoons (30 ml) olive oil

2 medium leeks, 2 cups (180 g),
white parts only, chopped

9 garlic cloves, peeled

2 cups (480 ml) low-sodium
vegetable broth

2 (9.9-ounce/280-g) jars artichoke
hearts in water, rinsed and drained

1 medium Russet potato (170 g),
cut into 1-inch (2.5 cm) chunks

6 fresh thyme sprigs, stemmed

2 teaspoons lemon juice

Sea salt, to taste

1. Heat oil in a large saucepan over medium heat. Add leeks and garlic; sauté for 5 minutes or until leeks are softened and translucent. Add broth, artichokes, potatoes, thyme, and 2 cups (480 ml) water. Cover and bring to a boil.

2. Reduce heat to medium-low; simmer, partially covered, for 20 to 25 minutes, or until potatoes are tender.

3. Place mixture into the Vitamix container. Add lemon juice and firmly secure the lid.

4. Select Variable 1.

5. Start machine and slowly increase speed to Variable 10.

6. Blend for 30 to 40 seconds.

7. Season to taste with sea salt, if desired.

Nutritional Information

Amount Per Serving: Calories 180, Total Fat 11g, Saturated Fat 1.5g, Cholesterol 5mg, Sodium 360mg, Total Carbohydrates 16g, Dietary Fiber 1g, Sugars 2g, Protein 5g

Crab Bisque

Preparation: 25 minutes | **Processing:** Pulsing plus 30–40 seconds | **Cook Time:** 30–35 minutes
Yield: 4¾ cups (1.1 l) soup and 2 cups (480 ml) relish (4 servings)

Relish:

1 medium tomato, 5 ounces (140 g), quartered

1 cup (155 g) corn kernels, fresh or frozen, thawed

1 small avocado, pitted and peeled

1 Tablespoon lime juice

¼ teaspoon salt

Dash of ground black pepper

Bisque:

1 Tablespoon extra virgin olive oil

1 cup (155 g) corn kernels, fresh or frozen, thawed

1 cup (160 g) chopped onion

1 cup (150 g) chopped yellow bell pepper

1½ cups (225 g) unpeeled, chopped Russet potato

¾ teaspoon sweet or hot smoked paprika,
plus additional for garnish

1 cup (240 ml) dry sherry

2 cups (480 ml) clam juice

2 cups (480 ml) 2% milk

12 ounces (340 g) crab meat, rinsed

½ teaspoon salt

1. To make the relish, place tomato, corn, avocado, lime juice, salt, and pepper into the Vitamix container in the order listed and firmly secure the lid.

2. Select Variable 1.

3. Pulse 3 to 4 times. Stop machine and remove lid. Scrape down the sides of the container with a spatula and firmly secure the lid. Repeat process until desired consistency is reached. Transfer to a bowl and set aside. Clean container.

4. To make the bisque, heat oil in a large saucepan over medium heat. Add corn, onion, and bell pepper and cook, stirring often, until the onion and pepper have softened, about 5 minutes.

5. Add potato and paprika and cook, stirring often, for 2 minutes. Add sherry and cook, scraping the bottom of the skillet to incorporate brown bits until the liquid has reduced slightly, about 5 minutes. Add clam juice and bring to a boil. Reduce heat and simmer, until the potatoes are tender, about 15 minutes. Remove from heat and let cool 15 minutes.

6. Transfer mixture to the Vitamix container and firmly secure the lid.

7. Select Variable 1.

8. Start machine and slowly increase speed to Variable 10.

9. Blend for 30 to 40 seconds, until desired consistency is reached.

10. Return purée to the saucepan. Stir in milk and crab meat. Cook, stirring occasionally, until heated through, 3 to 5 minutes.

11. Serve topped with relish and sprinkled with paprika.

Nutritional Information

Amount Per Serving: *Calories 460, Total Fat 13g, Saturated Fat 3g, Cholesterol 80mg, Sodium 1260mg, Total Carbohydrates 45g, Dietary Fiber 6g, Sugars 18g, Protein 25g*

Curried Cauliflower Soup

Preparation: 20 minutes | **Processing:** 45–50 seconds
Cook Time: 30 minutes | **Yield:** 7½ cups (1.8 l) (7 servings)

1 medium onion, 5 ounces (140 g),
rough chopped

1 medium tart apple, 7 ounces (200 g),
plus additional for garnish, cored
and quartered

1 Tablespoon curry powder

1 garlic clove, peeled

1 large head cauliflower, 6 cups (600 g),
chopped into 1-inch (2.5 cm) pieces

4 cups (960 ml) low-sodium
vegetable broth

1 teaspoon honey

1 teaspoon rice wine vinegar

Sea salt, to taste

1. Heat a large pot over medium-high heat. Add onion and a few Tablespoons of water. Sauté 5 to 7 minutes or until soft and golden, stirring frequently. Continue to add water, a few Tablespoons at a time, as needed to prevent the onions from sticking to the pan. Stir in apple, curry powder, and garlic. Cook an additional 2 minutes until curry turns deep yellow.

2. Add cauliflower and broth and bring to a simmer. Cover, reduce heat to medium-low, and simmer 20 minutes.

3. Transfer mixture to the Vitamix container and firmly secure the lid. Select Variable 1.

4. Start machine and slowly increase speed to Variable 8. Blend for 35 to 40 seconds.

5. Reduce speed to Variable 1 and remove lid plug.

6. Pour honey and vinegar through the lid plug opening. Replace lid plug and blend an additional 10 seconds.

7. Ladle soup into bowls and garnish with diced apple. Season to taste with sea salt, if desired.

Nutritional Information

Amount Per Serving: *Calories 60, Total Fat 0g, Saturated Fat 0g, Cholesterol 0mg, Sodium 110mg, Total Carbohydrate 14g, Dietary Fiber 3g, Sugars 7g, Protein 2g*

Garden Fresh Vegetable Soup

Preparation: 10 minutes | **Processing:** 5 minutes 45 seconds
Yield: 6½ cups (1.5 l) (6 servings)

1 cup (240 ml) hot water

1 (14-ounce/400-g)
can diced tomatoes

1 (10-ounce/285-g) package
frozen spinach, thawed

½ medium cucumber,
6 ounces (175 g), halved

1 medium carrot,
3 ounces (80 g), halved

1 stalk celery,
2½ ounces (75 g), halved

⅓ cup (30 g) broccoli florets

1 vegetable bouillon cube

2 garlic cloves, peeled

5–6 thin slices (10 g)
fresh ginger root

¼ teaspoon dried sage

¼ teaspoon ground cumin

¼ teaspoon dried basil

Dash of hot sauce

Sea salt, to taste

1. Place all ingredients into the Vitamix container in the order listed and firmly secure the lid.

2. Select Variable 1 or the Hot Soup program.

3. Start machine, slowly increase to its highest speed, and blend for 5 minutes 45 seconds, using the tamper to press the ingredients into the blades; or start machine and allow programmed cycle to complete, using the tamper to press the ingredients into the blades.

4. Season to taste with sea salt, if desired. Serve immediately.

Nutritional Information

Amount Per Serving: *Calories 45, Total Fat 0.5g, Saturated Fat 0g, Cholesterol 0mg, Sodium 360mg, Total Carbohydrates 9g, Dietary Fiber 3g, Sugars 4g, Protein 3g*

Thai Ginger Soup ♨

Preparation: 15 minutes | ***Processing:*** 5 minutes 45 seconds
Yield: 4½ cups (1.0 l) (4 servings)

2 cups (480 ml) water

1 carrot, 3 ounces (85 g), halved

1 slice cabbage, 3 ounces (85 g)
(about 1 cup)

1 stalk celery, halved

1 slice green bell pepper,
¾ ounce (20 g) (⅛ of a medium)

1 piece zucchini, 2 ounces (60 g)
(⅓ of a medium)

1 spring onion, halved

1 thin slice lemon, unpeeled

½ garlic clove, peeled

1 piece fresh ginger root,
½ ounce (15 g), unpeeled

¼ fresh jalapeño

½ cup (70 g) unsalted,
roasted cashews

⅓ cup (5 g) fresh cilantro leaves

1 teaspoon (5 g) honey

1 vegetable stock cube

1. Place all ingredients into the Vitamix container in the order listed and firmly secure the lid.

2. Select Variable 1 or the Hot Soup program.

3. Start machine, slowly increase to its highest speed, and blend for 5 minutes 45 seconds; or start machine and allow programmed cycle to complete.

4. Serve immediately.

Nutritional Information

Amount Per Serving: *Calories 130, Total Fat 9g, Saturated Fat 2g, Cholesterol 0mg, Sodium 290mg, Total Carbohydrate 12g, Dietary Fiber 2g, Sugars 5g, Protein 4g*

Root Vegetable Soup

Preparation: 20 minutes | **Processing:** 5 minutes 50 seconds
Cook Time: 6 minutes | **Yield:** 4 cups (960 ml)

1 Tablespoon extra virgin olive oil

⅓ cup (50 g) sliced onions

1 garlic clove, peeled and quartered

⅔ cup (85 g) chopped carrots

⅓ cup (50 g) peeled and
chopped parsnips

2 small red potatoes, cooked,
divided use

½ cup (65 g) peeled and
cubed turnips

1-inch (2.5 cm) piece of peeled,
fresh ginger root, rough chopped

2 Tablespoons (6 g) fresh dill weed

½ teaspoon salt

¼ teaspoon ground black pepper

1 cup (240 ml) low-sodium
chicken broth

1 cup (240 ml) half & half

1. In a small 8-inch (20-cm) nonstick skillet, heat olive oil over medium heat and add onions. Cook 4 minutes, stirring occasionally.

2. Add garlic and continue cooking, stirring occasionally, for 1 minute.

3. Place cooked onion mixture, carrots, parsnips, 1 red potato, turnips, ginger, dill, salt, pepper, broth, and half & half into the Vitamix container in the order listed and firmly secure the lid.

4. Select Variable 1 or the Hot Soup program.

5. Start machine, slowly increase to its highest speed, and blend for 5 minutes 45 seconds; or start machine and allow programmed cycle to complete.

6. Select Variable 2. Start machine and remove lid plug. Add remaining potato through the lid plug opening and secure lid plug.

7. Blend an additional 5 seconds or until smooth. Serve immediately.

Nutritional Information

Amount Per 1 Cup (240 ml) Serving: *Calories 200, Total Fat 11g, Saturated Fat 5g, Cholesterol 20mg, Sodium 500mg, Total Carbohydrate 24g, Dietary Fiber 3g, Sugars 4g, Protein 5g*

Chicken Potato Spinach Soup

Preparation: 15 minutes | **Processing:** 5 minutes 55 seconds – 6 minutes
Yield: 5¼ cups (1.2 l) (5 servings)

1 cup (240 ml) low-sodium chicken broth

1½ cups (360 ml) unsweetened soy or almond milk

¼ cup (40 g) chopped onion

3 medium Russet potatoes (640 g), baked and halved, divided use

⅛ teaspoon dried rosemary

1 Tablespoon spinach, cooked or frozen, thawed

5 ounces (140 g) skinless, boneless chicken breast, cooked and diced

Sea salt, to taste

1. Place broth, milk, onion, two potatoes, and rosemary into the Vitamix container in the order listed and firmly secure the lid.

2. Select Variable 1 or the Hot Soup program.

3. Start machine, slowly increase to its highest speed, and blend for 5 minutes 45 seconds; or start machine and allow programmed cycle to complete.

4. Reduce speed to Variable 1 and remove lid plug.

5. Add spinach, remaining potato, and chicken through the lid plug opening. Secure lid plug and blend an additional 10 to 15 seconds, or until desired consistency is reached.

6. Season to taste with sea salt, if desired.

Nutritional Information

Amount Per Serving: *Calories 180, Total Fat 5g, Saturated Fat 1g, Cholesterol 15mg, Sodium 280mg, Total Carbohydrate 24g, Dietary Fiber 2g, Sugars 5g, Protein 9g*

Dressings

__Easily adjust dressings and marinades__ to your own flavor profiles by changing up the herbs and spices. As chefs say, "walk through the garden" to see what you have on hand.

Dressings

SALADS / MARINADES

Orange Vanilla Vinaigrette

Preparation: 15 minutes | **Processing:** 20 seconds | **Yield:** 3 cups (720 ml)

2 oranges, peeled, halved, and seeded

1 Tablespoon apple cider vinegar

1½ teaspoons vanilla extract

1 Tablespoon honey

1 lemon, peeled, halved, and seeded

Dash of hot sauce

¼ teaspoon salt

⅛ teaspoon ground black pepper

1½ cups (360 ml) extra virgin olive oil

1. Place oranges, vinegar, vanilla, honey, lemon, hot sauce, salt, and pepper into the Vitamix container in the order listed and firmly secure the lid.

2. Select Variable 1.

3. Start machine and slowly increase speed to Variable 4.

4. Blend for 20 seconds or until smooth. Reduce speed to Variable 1 and remove the lid plug.

5. Slowly pour olive oil through the lid plug opening until emulsified.

Nutritional Information

Amount Per 2 Tablespoon (30 ml) Serving: *Calories 140, Total Fat 14g, Saturated Fat 2g, Cholesterol 0mg, Sodium 25mg, Total Carbohydrate 2g, Dietary Fiber 0g, Sugars 2g, Protein 0g*

Raspberry Vinaigrette

Preparation: 10 minutes | *Processing:* 30 seconds | *Yield:* 1¾ cups (420 ml)

¾ cup (180 ml) olive oil

¼ cup (60 ml) apple cider vinegar or raspberry vinegar

1 teaspoon salt

1 teaspoon dried basil

½ cup (60 g) raspberries, fresh or frozen unsweetened, thawed

¼ cup (60 ml) water

2 Tablespoons (30 ml) honey

1. Place olive oil, vinegar, salt, basil, raspberries, and water into the Vitamix container in the order listed and firmly secure the lid.

2. Select Variable 1.

3. Start machine and remove the lid plug. Add honey through the lid plug opening and secure lid plug.

4. Slowly increase speed to Variable 4.

5. Blend for 30 seconds.

Nutritional Information

Amount Per 2 Tablespoon (30 ml) Serving: Calories 120, Total Fat 12g, Saturated Fat 1.5g, Cholesterol 0mg, Sodium 170mg, Total Carbohydrate 4g, Dietary Fiber 0g, Sugars 2g, Protein 0g

Fresh Apple and Pear Dressing

Preparation: 10 minutes | ***Processing:*** 20 seconds
Cook Time: 4–6 minutes | ***Yield:*** 2½ cups (600 ml)

1 ripe apple, cored and chopped

1 ripe pear, cored and chopped

½ cup (100 g) granulated sugar

⅔ cup (160 ml) water

1 teaspoon fresh tarragon leaves

4 Tablespoons (60 ml) cider vinegar, divided use

3 Tablespoons (45 ml) fresh lemon juice, divided use

1. Place apple, pear, sugar, water, and tarragon in a medium saucepan and simmer, covered, over medium heat until very soft, about 4 to 6 minutes, depending on ripeness of fruit.

2. Let water evaporate. There should be about 1¾ cups (420 ml) fruit and liquid when finished cooking. Allow the mixture to cool.

3. Pour fruit mixture into the Vitamix container and firmly secure the lid.

4. Select Variable 1.

5. Start machine and slowly increase to its highest speed.

6. Blend for 20 seconds or until smooth.

7. Transfer mixture to a medium-size bowl. Whisk in 2 Tablespoons cider vinegar and 1½ Tablespoons lemon juice. Taste; dressing should be a pleasant blend of sweet and tart. If desired, add remaining cider vinegar and lemon juice.

Nutritional Information

Amount Per 2 Tablespoon (30 ml) Serving: *Calories 30, Total Fat 0g, Saturated Fat 0g, Cholesterol 0mg, Sodium 0mg, Total Carbohydrate 8g, Dietary Fiber 1g, Sugars 7g, Protein 0g*

Greek Salad Dressing

Preparation: 10 minutes | **Processing:** 20 seconds | **Yield:** 1½ cups (360 ml)

2 large lemons, peeled with white removed, halved, and seeded

¾ cup (180 ml) extra virgin olive oil

1½ teaspoons dried oregano leaves

2 garlic cloves, peeled

¾ teaspoon sugar

¼ teaspoon salt

⅛ teaspoon ground black pepper

⅓ cup (50 g) crumbled feta cheese

6 Kalamata olives, pitted

1. Place lemons, oil, oregano, garlic, sugar, salt, and pepper into the Vitamix container in the order listed and firmly secure the lid.

2. Select Variable 1.

3. Start machine and slowly increase speed to Variable 5.

4. Blend for 15 seconds or until smooth. Stop machine and remove lid. Add feta cheese and olives and firmly secure the lid.

5. Select Variable 1.

6. Start machine and slowly increase speed to Variable 3. Blend for 5 seconds. If necessary, scrape down the sides of the container with a spatula and blend for a few more seconds.

Nutritional Information

Amount Per 2 Tablespoon (30 ml) Serving: *Calories 150, Total Fat 16g, Saturated Fat 2.5g, Cholesterol 5mg, Sodium 125mg, Total Carbohydrate 2g, Dietary Fiber 0g, Sugars 1g, Protein 1g*

Tomato Vinaigrette

Preparation: 10 minutes | **Processing:** 20 seconds | **Yield:** 2 cups (480 ml)

½ cup (120 ml) white balsamic vinegar

¼ cup (60 ml) water

¾ cup plus 2 Tablespoons (210 ml) extra virgin olive oil

½ teaspoon salt

¼ teaspoon ground black pepper

6 Tablespoons (20 g) chopped fresh chives

1 Roma tomato, halved

1. Place all ingredients into the Vitamix container in the order listed and firmly secure the lid.

2. Select Variable 1.

3. Start machine and slowly increase speed to Variable 5.

4. Blend for 20 seconds, or until emulsified.

Nutritional Information

Amount Per 2 Tablespoon (30 ml) Serving: *Calories 110, Total Fat 12g, Saturated Fat 1.5g, Cholesterol 0mg, Sodium 150mg, Total Carbohydrate 1g, Dietary Fiber 0g, Sugars 1g, Protein 0g*

Caesar Salad Dressing

Preparation: 10 minutes | *Processing:* 35 seconds | *Yield:* 4 cups (960 ml)

6 large eggs

2 Tablespoons (30 ml) red wine vinegar

1½ small garlic cloves, peeled

½ cup plus 1 Tablespoon (135 ml) lemon juice

1 cup (100 g) grated Parmesan cheese

½ teaspoon salt

1 Tablespoon plus 1½ teaspoons anchovy filets

⅓ teaspoon dry mustard

1 cup plus 2 Tablespoons (270 ml) extra virgin olive oil

1. Place eggs, vinegar, garlic, lemon juice, Parmesan, salt, anchovy, and mustard into the Vitamix container in the order listed and firmly secure the lid.

2. Select Variable 1.

3. Start machine and slowly increase speed to Variable 5.

4. Blend for 25 seconds, or until smooth. Reduce speed to Variable 1 and remove the lid plug.

5. Slowly pour olive oil through the lid plug opening and blend an additional 10 seconds.

Nutritional Information

Amount Per 2 Tablespoon (30 ml) Serving: Calories 90, Total Fat 10g, Saturated Fat 2g, Cholesterol 35mg, Sodium 85mg, Total Carbohydrate 1g, Dietary Fiber 0g, Sugars 0g, Protein 2g

Fresh Herb Ranch Dressing

Preparation: 15 minutes | **Processing:** 20 seconds | **Yield:** 2½ cups (600 ml)

1 cup (240 g) real mayonnaise

1 cup (240 g) sour cream

¾ cup (20 g) mixed fresh herbs (dill, marjoram, basil, etc.)

2 Tablespoons (10 g) chopped green onion

2 Tablespoons (30 ml) white vinegar

½ teaspoon garlic powder

½ teaspoon salt

¼ teaspoon ground black pepper

1. Place all ingredients into the Vitamix container in the order listed and firmly secure the lid.

2. Select Variable 1.

3. Start machine and slowly increase speed to Variable 5.

4. Blend for 20 seconds, or until smooth, using the tamper to press the ingredients into the blades.

Nutritional Information

Amount Per 2 Tablespoon (30 ml) Serving: *Calories 100, Total Fat 11g, Saturated Fat 2.5g, Cholesterol 10mg, Sodium 125mg, Total Carbohydrate 1g, Dietary Fiber 0g, Sugars 0g, Protein 0g*

Green Goddess Dressing

Preparation: 10 minutes | *Processing:* 25 seconds | *Yield:* 2 cups (600 ml)

1 cup (240 g) mayonnaise

½ cup (110 g) sour cream

2 lemons, peeled and seeded,
or 2 Tablespoons (30 ml) lemon juice

½ cup (30 g) fresh tarragon leaves

½ cup (30 g) fresh chopped parsley

½ cup (30 g) fresh chopped chives

2 garlic cloves, peeled and minced

2 anchovies

½ teaspoon salt

1. Place all ingredients into the Vitamix container in the order listed and firmly secure the lid.

2. Select Variable 1.

3. Start machine and slowly increase speed to Variable 10.

4. Blend for 25 seconds.

Nutritional Information

Amount Per 2 Tablespoon (30 ml) Serving: *Calories 100, Total Fat 10g, Saturated Fat 2g, Cholesterol 10mg, Sodium 135mg, Total Carbohydrate 1g, Dietary Fiber 0g, Sugars 0g, Protein 1g*

Citrus Honey Marinade

Preparation: 25 minutes | ***Processing:*** 20 seconds | ***Yield:*** 1 cup (240 ml)

¾ cup (180 ml) pineapple juice

2 Tablespoons (30 ml) honey

1 Tablespoon fresh lime juice

1 teaspoon lime zest

2 garlic cloves, peeled

½ teaspoon cumin seeds

2 teaspoons chopped cilantro leaves

½ jalapeño (15 g), seeded

1. Place all ingredients into the Vitamix container in the order listed and firmly secure the lid.

2. Select Variable 1.

3. Start machine and slowly increase speed to Variable 2.

4. Blend for 20 seconds.

Nutritional Information

Amount Per 2 Tablespoon (30 ml) Serving: *Calories 30, Total Fat 0g, Saturated Fat 0g, Cholesterol 0mg, Sodium 0mg, Total Carbohydrate 8g, Dietary Fiber 0g, Sugars 6g, Protein 0g*

Parmesan Balsamic Vinaigrette

Preparation: 10 minutes | ***Processing:*** 20 seconds | ***Yield:*** 1½ cups (360 ml)

¼ cup (60 ml) balsamic vinegar

1 lemon, peeled

1 small garlic clove, peeled

½ teaspoon salt

3 Tablespoons (5 g)
fresh basil leaves

3 Tablespoons (5 g)
fresh thyme leaves

½ cup (40 g) finely grated
Parmesan cheese

¼ teaspoon ground
black pepper

1 cup (240 ml) extra virgin
olive oil, divided use

1. Place vinegar, lemon, garlic, salt, basil, thyme, Parmesan, pepper, and ½ cup (120 ml) olive oil into the Vitamix container in the order listed and firmly secure the lid.

2. Select Variable 1.

3. Start machine and slowly increase speed to Variable 6.

4. Blend for 5 seconds. Reduce speed to Variable 1 and remove lid plug.

5. Pour remaining ½ cup (120 ml) oil through the lid plug opening in a slow, steady stream, and secure lid plug.

6. Slowly increase speed to Variable 8.

7. Blend for 15 seconds, or until emulsified.

Nutritional Information

Amount Per 2 Tablespoon (30 ml) Serving: *Calories 190, Total Fat 20g, Saturated Fat 3g, Cholesterol 5mg, Sodium 150mg, Total Carbohydrate 2g, Dietary Fiber 0g, Sugars 1g, Protein 1g*

Dips & Spreads

Entertaining guests is easy with crowd-pleasing appetizers and well-dressed sandwich platters. Pair these with our cocktail recipes, and you can be ready for an impromptu party in minutes.

Dips & Spreads

APPETIZERS / SANDWICHES

Peanut Butter

Preparation: 10 minutes | **Processing:** 1 minute 30 seconds
Yield: 2 cups (480 ml)

4 cups (590 g) unsalted dry roasted peanuts

1. Place nuts into the Vitamix container and firmly secure the lid.

2. Select Variable 1.

3. Start machine and slowly increase to its highest speed.

4. Use the tamper to press the ingredients into the blades.

5. In 1 minute, you will hear a high-pitched chugging sound. Once the butter begins to flow freely through the blades, reduce speed to Variable 7.

6. Blend for 30 seconds.

7. Store refrigerated in an airtight container for up to 1 week. It can also be frozen for longer storage.

Nutritional Information

Amount Per 2 Tablespoon (30 ml) Serving: *Calories 210, Total Fat 18g, Saturated Fat 2.5g, Cholesterol 0mg, Sodium 0mg, Total Carbohydrate 8g, Dietary Fiber 3g, Sugars 2g, Protein 9g*

Nut Butters & Spreads

Homemade nut butters taste so much fresher and more flavorful than store-bought varieties and contain no preservatives. Use unflavored versions made with ground nuts like peanuts, almonds, cashews and more to make better sandwiches, vegetable dips, or to add rich flavor to noodle dishes and stews.

Sweetened nut butters are perfect as a dip for fresh fruit, topping for muffins and breakfast breads, or atop crackers with sliced bananas as a healthy snack. They're also delicious as a filling for sandwich cookies and blended into creamy fruit smoothies. Try sweeteners like honey, maple syrup, cinnamon, agave, vanilla, raisins, or pitted dates.

Almond Butter

Preparation: 10 minutes | **Processing:** 2 minutes 30 seconds | **Yield:** 2 cups (480 ml)

4 cups (590 g) raw almonds

¼ cup (60 ml) canola oil

1. Place almonds into the Vitamix container and firmly secure the lid.

2. Select Variable 1.

3. Start machine and slowly increase to its highest speed.

4. Blend for 2 minutes, using the tamper to press the ingredients into the blades.

5. Stop machine and remove the lid plug. Add oil through the lid plug opening.

6. Select Variable 1.

7. Start machine and slowly increase speed to Variable 8.

8. Blend for 30 seconds.

9. Store refrigerated in an airtight container for up to 1 week. It can also be frozen for longer storage.

Nutritional Information

Amount Per 2 Tablespoon (30 ml) Serving: *Calories 240, Total Fat 21g, Saturated Fat 1.5g, Cholesterol 0mg, Sodium 0mg, Total Carbohydrate 7g, Dietary Fiber 4g, Sugars 2g, Protein 7g*

Red Pepper Walnut Pesto

Preparation: 15 minutes | **Processing:** 30 seconds
Bake Time: 15–20 minutes | **Yield:** 2 cups (480 ml)

1 large red bell pepper,
6 ounces (270 g)

2 medium garlic cloves, peeled

¾ cup (75 g) walnuts, toasted

½ cup (30 g) sun-dried tomatoes

⅔ cup (20 g) fresh basil leaves

½ cup (50 g) grated
Parmesan cheese

½ teaspoon salt

¼ teaspoon ground
black pepper

½ cup (120 ml) olive oil

1. Preheat oven to 400°F (200°C). Halve and trim red pepper and place skin side down on the oven rack. Roast 15 to 20 minutes, or until skin is well shriveled but not blackened. Place pepper in a plastic bag for 15 minutes to steam.

2. Place garlic cloves in a medium saucepan, add cold water to cover, and bring to a boil. Reduce heat and simmer for 5 minutes or until soft enough to pierce with a fork. Remove using a slotted spoon and set aside to drain.

3. Place all ingredients into the Vitamix container in the order listed and firmly secure the lid.

4. Select Variable 1.

5. Start machine and slowly increase speed to Variable 3. Blend for 30 seconds, or until desired consistency is reached, using the tamper to press the ingredients into the blades.

Nutritional Information

Amount Per 2 Tablespoon (30 ml) Serving: *Calories 60, Total Fat 6g, Saturated Fat 1g, Cholesterol 0mg, Sodium 55mg, Total Carbohydrate 1g, Dietary Fiber 0g, Sugars 0g, Protein 1g*

Lemon Gremolata Dip

Preparation: 15 minutes | **Processing:** 20–25 seconds | **Yield:** 2½ cups (600 ml)

1 cup (240 g) sour cream

1 cup (240 g) plain
Greek-style yogurt

1 cup (60 g) fresh parsley,
washed, dried, stems removed

¼ cup (25 g) lemon peel

¼ lemon, peeled and seeded

1 teaspoon agave

2 garlic cloves, peeled

½ teaspoon ground coriander

¼ teaspoon salt

⅛ teaspoon ground
black pepper

1. Place all ingredients into the Vitamix container in the order listed and firmly secure the lid.

2. Select Variable 1.

3. Start machine and slowly increase to its highest speed.

4. Blend for 20 to 25 seconds, or until smooth.

Nutritional Information

Amount Per ¼ Cup (60 ml) Serving: *Calories 90, Total Fat 6g, Saturated Fat 4.5g, Cholesterol 20mg, Sodium 75mg, Total Carbohydrate 3g, Dietary Fiber 1g, Sugars 2g, Protein 3g*

California Salsa

Preparation: 15 minutes | *Processing:* Pulsing | *Yield:* 4 cups (960 ml)

½ medium onion (45 g), peeled, or ⅓ cup chopped onion

1 jalapeño, seeds and membranes removed

¼ cup (5 g) fresh cilantro leaves

½ lemon or lime, juiced

½ teaspoon salt

6 ripe Roma tomatoes, quartered (24 quarters), divided use

1. Place onion, jalapeño, cilantro, lime, salt, and six of the tomato quarters into the Vitamix container in the order listed and firmly secure the lid.

2. Select Variable 5. Pulse 5 times if onion has not been chopped by hand. Pulse 2 to 3 times if starting with chopped onion.

3. Add the remaining tomato quarters through the lid plug opening. Pulse 10 to 12 times, or until desired consistency is reached, using the tamper to press the ingredients into the blades.

4. Do not overmix, leave chunky. Serve with tortilla chips.

Nutritional Information

Amount Per 2 Tablespoon (30 ml) Serving: Calories 5, Total Fat 0g, Saturated Fat 0g, Cholesterol 0mg, Sodium 40mg, Total Carbohydrate 1g, Dietary Fiber 0g, Sugars 1g, Protein 0g

Guacamole

Preparation: 10 minutes | **Processing:** Pulsing
Yield: 2½ cups (600 ml)

2 ripe avocados, halved, pitted, and peeled

1 Roma tomato, quartered

½ cup (10 g) fresh cilantro leaves

¼ cup (40 g) chopped red onion

2 Tablespoons (30 ml) lemon juice

½ teaspoon kosher salt

1. Place all ingredients into the Vitamix container in the order listed and firmly secure the lid.

2. Select Variable 4.

3. Pulse 5 to 6 times, or until ingredients are mixed, using the tamper to press the ingredients into the blades.

4. Do not overmix. Leave chunky. Serve with tortilla chips.

Nutritional Information

Amount Per 2 Tablespoon (30 ml) Serving: *Calories 25, Total Fat 2g, Saturated Fat 0g, Cholesterol 0mg, Sodium 50mg, Total Carbohydrate 2g, Dietary Fiber 1g, Sugars 0g, Protein 0g*

Chef's Note

For a spicy *guacamole, add ½ jalapeño pepper during Step 1.*

Hummus

Preparation: 15 minutes | ***Processing:*** 45–55 seconds | ***Yield:*** 4 cups (960 ml)

2 (15-ounce/425-g) cans chickpeas (garbanzos),
one drained, one with liquid

¼ cup (35 g) raw sesame seeds

1 Tablespoon olive oil

¼ cup (60 ml) lemon juice

¼ cup (60 ml) water

1 garlic clove, peeled

1 teaspoon ground cumin

½ teaspoon salt

1. Place all ingredients into the Vitamix container in the order listed and firmly secure the lid.

2. Select Variable 1.

3. Start machine and slowly increase to its highest speed.

4. Blend for 45 to 55 seconds, or until desired consistency is reached.

Nutritional Information

Amount Per 2 Tablespoon (30 ml) Serving: *Calories 35, Total Fat 1.5g, Saturated Fat 0g, Cholesterol 0mg, Sodium 110mg, Total Carbohydrate 4g, Dietary Fiber 1g, Sugars 0g, Protein 1g*

Spinach Artichoke Dip

Preparation: 20 minutes | **Processing:** 25 seconds
Bake Time: 20–25 minutes | **Yield:** 2¾ cups (660 ml) (22 servings)

½ cup (120 g) light mayonnaise

½ cup (120 g) low-fat sour cream

¼-inch (½ cm) slice lemon, peeled

1 (10-ounce/285-g) package
frozen spinach, thawed, and drained

⅛ teaspoon salt

⅛ teaspoon ground black pepper

1 garlic clove, peeled

¼ cup (50 g) grated
Parmesan cheese

½ cup (85 g) canned
artichoke hearts, drained

1. Preheat oven to 350°F (180°C).

2. Place mayonnaise, sour cream, lemon, spinach, salt, pepper, garlic, and Parmesan into the Vitamix container in the order listed and firmly secure the lid.

3. Select Variable 1.

4. Start machine and slowly increase speed to Variable 6.

5. Blend for 15 seconds. While machine is running, remove the lid plug and add artichokes through the lid plug opening. Secure lid plug and blend an additional 10 seconds.

6. Pour into an oven-safe dish and bake uncovered 20 to 25 minutes, or until bubbly.

Nutritional Information

Amount Per 2 Tablespoon (30 ml) Serving: Calories 35, Total Fat 2.5g, Saturated Fat 1g, Cholesterol 5mg, Sodium 115mg, Total Carbohydrate 2g, Dietary Fiber 0g, Sugars 1g, Protein 1g

Tuscan Bean Dip

Preparation: 15 minutes | **Processing:** 20 seconds plus Pulsing
Yield: 3 cups (720 ml) (24 servings)

2 (15-ounce/425-g) cans cannellini beans, drained, divided use

2 Tablespoons (30 ml) fresh lemon juice

¼ cup (60 ml) water

1 Tablespoon fresh oregano, or ½ teaspoon dried oregano

2 garlic cloves, peeled

½ teaspoon ground cumin

2 scallions, halved

¼ cup (30 g) sun-dried tomatoes, finely chopped, rehydrated, drained

Several dashes of hot sauce

Sea salt, to taste

1. Place one can drained beans, lemon juice, water, oregano, garlic, and cumin into the Vitamix container in the order listed and firmly secure the lid.

2. Select Variable 1.

3. Start machine and slowly increase speed to Variable 6.

4. Blend for 20 seconds.

5. Add remaining can of beans, scallions, sun-dried tomatoes, and hot sauce into the Vitamix container in the order listed and firmly secure the lid.

6. Select Variable 6.

7. Pulse 10 times.

8. Season to taste with sea salt, if desired.

Nutritional Information

Amount Per 2 Tablespoon (30 ml) Serving: *Calories 40, Total Fat 0g, Saturated Fat 0g, Cholesterol 0mg, Sodium 115mg, Total Carbohydrate 7g, Dietary Fiber 2g, Sugars 1g, Protein 3g*

Southwest Black Bean Dip

Preparation: 15 minutes | **Processing:** 30–40 seconds | **Yield:** 4 cups (960 ml)

½ cup (120 ml) water

2 Tablespoons (30 ml) balsamic vinegar

2 Tablespoons (30 ml) fresh lemon juice

4 Tablespoons fresh cilantro leaves plus additional for garnish

4 garlic cloves, peeled

2 (15-ounce/425-g) cans no salt added black beans, rinsed and drained

2 teaspoons ground cumin

1 teaspoon chili powder

Dash of ground black pepper

1. Place all ingredients into the Vitamix container in the order listed and firmly secure the lid.

2. Select Variable 1.

3. Start machine and slowly increase speed to Variable 7.

4. Blend for 30 to 40 seconds, using the tamper to press the ingredients into the blades.

5. Garnish with chopped fresh cilantro and serve with tortilla chips or fresh vegetables.

Nutritional Information

Amount Per 2 Tablespoon (30 ml) Serving: *Calories 25, Total Fat 0g, Saturated Fat 0g, Cholesterol 0mg, Sodium 5mg, Total Carbohydrate 5g, Dietary Fiber 2g, Sugars 0g, Protein 2*

Citrus Fruit Dip

Preparation: 15 minutes | **Processing:** 15 seconds | **Yield:** 3½ cups (840 ml) (28 servings)

3 cups (720 g) plain unsweetened soy yogurt,
strained to remove excess moisture

¼ cup (60 ml) honey

¼ lime, peeled

⅛ orange, peeled

½-inch (1½ cm) square piece of lime peel,
or 1 Tablespoon lime zest

½-inch (1½ cm) square piece of orange peel,
or 1 Tablespoon orange zest

1. Place all ingredients into the Vitamix container in the order listed
   and firmly secure the lid.

2. Select Variable 1.

3. Start machine and slowly increase speed to Variable 10.

4. Blend for 15 seconds.

5. Serve as a dip with fresh fruit or layer with granola and fruit for
   a delicious breakfast parfait.

Nutritional Information

Amount Per 2 Tablespoon (30 ml) Serving: *Calories 25, Total Fat 0.5g,
Saturated Fat 0g, Cholesterol 0mg, Sodium 0mg, Total Carbohydrate 3g,
Dietary Fiber 0g, Sugars 3g, Protein 1g*

Chef's Note

We've served this chutney with toasted baguette slices, topped with cream cheese. Also makes a sweet garnish for fish and pork dishes.

Dried Apricot Chutney

Preparation: 10 minutes | **Processing:** 5 seconds
Cook Time: 15–20 minutes | **Yield:** 2 cups (480 ml)

6 ounces (170 g) red pepper, quartered and seeded

1-inch (2½ cm) piece of fresh ginger root, peeled

1 (7-ounce/200-g) bag dried apricots, about 30 apricots

½ cup (120 ml) distilled vinegar

⅓ cup (65 g) granulated sugar

1. Place red pepper, ginger, and apricots into the Vitamix container in the order listed and firmly secure the lid.

2. Select Variable 1.

3. Start machine and slowly increase speed to Variable 3. Blend for 5 seconds, using the tamper to press the ingredients into the blades.

4. Transfer mixture to a 2-quart saucepan. Add vinegar, sugar, and ½ cup (120 ml) water. Mix well.

5. Bring to a boil over medium-high heat, stirring occasionally. Reduce heat to medium-low and simmer until thickened, about 15 to 20 minutes, stirring often to prevent sticking.

6. Pour into storage containers and cool to room temperature. Cover and chill until needed.

Nutritional Information

Amount Per ¼ Cup (60 ml) Serving: Calories 100, Total Fat 0g, Saturated Fat 0g, Cholesterol 0mg, Sodium 0mg, Total Carbohydrate 25g, Dietary Fiber 3g, Sugars 20g, Protein 1g

Sauces

Wake up pastas and proteins with fresh, all-natural sauces. Explore delicious recipes for savory pastas, beautifully garnished desserts, and more.

Sauces

PASTAS / MEATS

Kale and Basil Pesto

Preparation: 10 minutes | **Processing:** 30 seconds | **Yield:** 1¾ cups (420 ml)

1 cup (240 ml) olive oil

1 cup (100 g) grated Parmesan cheese

3 medium garlic cloves, peeled

2 cups (80 g) fresh basil leaves

2 cups (135 g) fresh kale leaves

3 Tablespoons (25 g) pine nuts

¼ teaspoon salt

Pinch of ground black pepper

1. Place all ingredients into the Vitamix container in the order listed and firmly secure the lid.

2. Select Variable 1.

3. Start machine and slowly increase speed to Variable 3.

4. Blend for 30 seconds, or until desired consistency is reached.

Nutritional Information

Amount Per 2 Tablespoon (30 ml) Serving: *Calories 190, Total Fat 19g, Saturated Fat 3.5g, Cholesterol 5mg, Sodium 125mg, Total Carbohydrate 2g, Dietary Fiber 0g, Sugars 0g, Protein 3g*

Chef's Note

We've plated *Fresh Tomato Sauce beneath a bed of sautéed spinach and grilled chicken.*

Fresh Tomato Sauce

Preparation: 15 minutes | **Processing:** 1 minute
Cook Time: 35–40 minutes | **Yield:** 3½ cups (840 ml)

6 medium Roma tomatoes (400 g), halved

¼ cup (40 g) chopped onion

½ cup (65 g) chopped carrot

2 Tablespoons (30 g) tomato paste

1 garlic clove, peeled

½ teaspoon dried basil

½ teaspoon dried oregano

½ teaspoon fresh lemon juice

½ teaspoon firmly packed brown sugar

¼ teaspoon salt, plus more to taste

Ground black pepper, to taste

1. Place all ingredients into the Vitamix container in the order listed and firmly secure the lid.

2. Select Variable 1 or the Purée program.

3. Start machine, slowly increase to its highest speed, and blend for 1 minute; or start machine and allow programmed cycle to complete.

4. Pour into a saucepan and simmer for 35 to 40 minutes over medium heat. Season to taste with additional salt and pepper.

Nutritional Information

Amount Per ½ Cup (120 ml) Serving: *Calories 25, Total Fat 0g, Saturated Fat 0g, Cholesterol 0mg, Sodium 110mg, Total Carbohydrate 5g, Dietary Fiber 1g, Sugars 3g, Protein 1g*

Roasted Vegetable Sauce ⓩ

Preparation: 20 minutes | **Processing:** 1 minute 5 seconds
Bake Time: 20 minutes | **Yield:** 6 servings

2 pounds (910 g) Roma
tomatoes, halved

3 garlic cloves, peeled

½ large carrot (70 g), halved

1½ cups (145 g)
button mushrooms

1 wedge red onion, peeled,
1½ inches (4 cm) thick

3 Tablespoons (45 ml)
extra virgin olive oil

1 teaspoon salt

¼ teaspoon ground
black pepper

1 (6-ounce/170-g)
can tomato paste

¼ cup (5 g) firmly packed
fresh basil leaves

¼ cup (5 g) firmly packed
fresh oregano leaves

1. Preheat oven to 450°F (230°C). Place tomatoes, garlic, carrot, mushrooms, and onion on an 11-inch x 17-inch (28-cm x 43-cm) cookie sheet. Drizzle with olive oil and sprinkle with salt and pepper. Roast for 20 minutes or until tomatoes are very tender, stirring mushrooms and garlic once.

2. Place all vegetables, liquid from the pan, and tomato paste into the Vitamix container and firmly secure the lid.

3. Select Variable 1 or the Purée program.

4. Start machine, slowly increase to its highest speed, and blend for 1 minute; or start machine and allow programmed cycle to complete.

5. Add basil and oregano to the Vitamix container and firmly secure the lid.

6. Select Variable 1.

7. Start machine and slowly increase speed to Variable 3.

8. Blend an additional 5 seconds. Serve over pasta.

Nutritional Information

Amount Per Serving: *Calories 140, Total Fat 7g, Saturated Fat 1g, Cholesterol 0mg, Sodium 500mg, Total Carbohydrate 16g, Dietary Fiber 4g, Sugars 9g, Protein 3g*

Green Curry Sauce

Preparation: 10 minutes | **Processing:** 15 seconds | **Yield:** 1½ cups (360 ml)

2 teaspoons sesame oil

¼ cup (25 g) peeled and chopped fresh ginger root

2 garlic cloves, peeled and sliced

¼ cup (60 ml) dry white wine

1 Tablespoon lime juice

2 teaspoons green curry paste

1 (13½-ounce/385-ml) can coconut milk

½ teaspoon fish sauce

½ cup (10 g) fresh cilantro leaves

Freshly ground kosher salt, to taste

Ground black pepper, to taste

Freshly squeezed lime juice, to taste

1. In a small saucepan, heat sesame oil over medium heat. Add ginger and garlic and sauté for 30 seconds. Add white wine and lime juice and reduce to almost dry. Add curry paste, coconut milk, and fish sauce, and reduce to 1 cup (240 ml) liquid. Let cool 10 minutes.

2. Place the cooked mixture, cilantro, and other optional seasonings into the Vitamix container and firmly secure the lid.

3. Select Variable 1.

4. Start machine and slowly increase to its highest speed.

5. Blend for 15 seconds.

Nutritional Information

Amount Per ¼ Cup (60 ml) Serving: *Calories 70, Total Fat 6g, Saturated Fat 4g, Cholesterol 0mg, Sodium 95mg, Total Carbohydrate 3g, Dietary Fiber 0g, Sugars 0g, Protein 0g*

Chef's Note

Serve with your favorite grilled meat or vegetable skewers.

Thai Peanut Sauce

Preparation: 15 minutes | **Processing:** 1 minute | **Yield:** 4 servings

1 (16-ounce/480-ml) can light coconut milk

2 Tablespoons (30 ml) soy sauce

2 Tablespoons (30 ml) rice wine vinegar

2 garlic cloves, peeled

1 teaspoon firmly packed brown sugar

1 teaspoon sesame oil

½ jalapeño pepper, seeds removed

1 cup (145 g) cocktail peanuts

1. Place all ingredients into the Vitamix container in the order listed and firmly secure the lid.

2. Select Variable 1 or the Purée program.

3. Start machine, slowly increase to its highest speed, and blend for 1 minute; or start machine and allow programmed cycle to complete.

Nutritional Information

Amount Per Serving: Calories 370, Total Fat 32g, Saturated Fat 10g, Cholesterol 0mg, Sodium 670mg, Total Carbohydrate 14g, Dietary Fiber 3g, Sugars 5g, Protein 10g

Tahini

Preparation: 10 minutes | **Processing:** 30 seconds | **Yield:** 1½ cups (360 ml) (6 servings)

½ cup (120 ml) rice bran oil or peanut oil

1 Tablespoon black sesame oil

3 Tablespoons (45 ml) rice wine vinegar

3 Tablespoons (45 ml) soy sauce

1 Tablespoon rice wine or saké

1 cup (130 g) white sesame seeds, toasted

2 Tablespoons (25 g) fine sugar

1. Place all ingredients into the Vitamix container in the order listed and secure lid.

2. Select Variable 1.

3. Start machine and slowly increase speed to Variable 8.

4. Blend for 30 seconds.

5. Store refrigerated in an airtight jar.

Nutritional Information

Amount Per Serving: *Calories 330, Total Fat 31g, Saturated Fat 5g, Cholesterol 0mg, Sodium 580mg, Total Carbohydrate 11g, Dietary Fiber 3g, Sugars 5g, Protein 4g*

Spicy Mango Sauce

Preparation: 15 minutes | **Processing:** 15 seconds | **Cook Time:** 10 – 15 minutes
Yield: 1¾ cups (420 ml) (14 servings)

2 Tablespoons (30 ml) canola oil

2½ ounces (70 g) onion, rough chopped

5½ ounces (155 g) red bell pepper,
seeded and rough chopped

3½ ounces (100 g) tomato, rough chopped

¾ cup (180 g) hot mango chutney

1. Heat oil in a medium-size saucepan over medium heat. Add onion and bell pepper. Cover and cook 5 to 7 minutes. Add tomato. Cover and cook 5 to 7 minutes. Add chutney, stirring to heat through. Cook for 1 to 2 minutes.

2. Place mixture into the Vitamix container and firmly secure the lid.

3. Select Variable 1.

4. Start machine and slowly increase speed to Variable 5.

5. Blend for 15 seconds.

6. Serve warm with grilled tofu or fish.

Nutritional Information

Amount Per 2 Tablespoon (30 ml) Serving: *Calories 60, Total Fat 3.5g, Saturated Fat 0g, Cholesterol 0mg, Sodium 140mg, Total Carbohydrate 8g, Dietary Fiber 1g, Sugars 1g, Protein 0g*

Cheese Sauce

Preparation: 15 minutes | ***Processing:*** 4–5 minutes | ***Yield:*** 2½ cups (600 ml)

¼ cup (60 g) butter

¼ cup (30 g) all-purpose flour

¼ teaspoon salt

1⅓ cups (320 ml) milk

½ teaspoon yellow mustard

1½ cups (175 g) cubed American cheese
or other mild yellow cheese

1. Place butter, flour, salt, milk, and mustard into the Vitamix container in the order listed and firmly secure the lid.

2. Select Variable 1.

3. Start machine and slowly increase speed to Variable 8.

4. Blend for 4 minutes, or until heavy steam escapes from the vented lid.

5. Reduce speed to Variable 1 and remove the lid plug. Add cheese through the lid plug opening.

6. Secure lid plug and blend an additional 30 seconds.

Nutritional Information

Amount Per ¼ Cup (60 ml) Serving: *Calories 150, Total Fat 12g, Saturated Fat 7g, Cholesterol 35mg, Sodium 200mg, Total Carbohydrate 4g, Dietary Fiber 0g, Sugars 2g, Protein 5g*

Breads & Batters

For breakfast or dessert, these warm sweet breads will delight family and guests. Pair them with homemade Butter (Kitchen Basics) and a cup of Mocha Spiced Hot Cocoa (Beverages) for a relaxing treat.

Breads & Batters

PANCAKES / MUFFINS / BREADS

Carrot Raisin Muffins

Preparation: 20 minutes | ***Processing:*** 25 seconds
Bake Time: 20–25 minutes | ***Yield:*** 12 muffins

1⅔ cups (200 g) self-rising flour

½ teaspoon baking soda

1 teaspoon ground cinnamon

1 teaspoon pumpkin pie spice

1 cup (165 g) raisins

¾ cup (100 g) chopped carrots

2 large eggs

¾ cup (150 g) granulated sugar

⅔ cup (160 ml) light olive oil

1. Preheat oven to 350°F (180°C). Spray a 12-muffin tin with cooking spray or line with cupcake papers.

2. Place flour, baking soda, cinnamon, and pumpkin pie spice in a medium-size mixing bowl and stir lightly. Stir in raisins and set aside.

3. Place carrots into the Vitamix container and firmly secure the lid.

4. Select Variable 2.

5. Start machine. Blend for 5 seconds or until very finely chopped. Stop machine and remove lid.

6. Add eggs, sugar, and oil to the carrots in the Vitamix container and firmly secure the lid.

7. Select Variable 1.

8. Start machine and slowly increase speed to Variable 6.

9. Blend for 20 seconds until thick and creamy.

10. Pour carrot mixture into flour mixture and fold by hand to combine. Spoon the mixture into prepared muffin tin.

11. Bake for 20 to 25 minutes until golden brown. Transfer to a wire rack to cool before serving.

Nutritional Information

Amount Per Serving: *Calories 270, Total Fat 13g, Saturated Fat 2g, Cholesterol 30mg, Sodium 300mg, Total Carbohydrate 37g, Dietary Fiber 1g, Sugars 23g, Protein 3g*

Lemon Ginger Muffins

Preparation: 30 minutes | **Processing:** 30 seconds
Bake Time: 15–20 minutes | **Yield:** 12 muffins

2 cups (250 g) all-purpose flour

1 Tablespoon plus 2 teaspoons freshly grated
lemon zest, divided use

1¾ teaspoons baking powder

¼ teaspoon salt

¾ cup (150 g) granulated sugar, divided use

¼ cup (60 g) crystallized ginger, small pieces

⅓ cup (80 g) butter, softened

1 large egg

¾ cup (180 ml) milk

3 Tablespoons (45 g) butter, melted

1 Tablespoon freshly squeezed lemon juice

1. Preheat oven to 350°F (180°C). Spray a 12-muffin tin with cooking spray or line with cupcake papers; set aside.

2. In a medium-size mixing bowl, stir together flour, 1 Tablespoon lemon zest, baking powder, and salt; set aside.

3. Place ½ cup (100 g) sugar and crystallized ginger into the Vitamix container and firmly secure the lid.

4. Select Variable 1.

5. Start machine and slowly increase speed to Variable 3.

6. Blend for 5 seconds. Stop machine and remove lid. Add softened butter to the Vitamix container and firmly secure the lid.

7. Select Variable 1.

8. Start machine and slowly increase speed to Variable 4.

9. Blend for 10 seconds. Stop machine and scrape sides of the container with a spatula.

10. Add egg and milk to the Vitamix container and firmly secure the lid.

11. Select Variable 1.

12. Start machine and slowly increase speed to Variable 5.

13. Blend for 15 seconds.

14. Pour wet mixture into dry ingredients and stir by hand to combine.

15. Spoon ¼ cup (60 ml) batter into each muffin cup. Bake until a toothpick inserted into the center comes out clean and edges are very lightly browned, about 15 to 20 minutes.

16. Meanwhile, in a small bowl, stir together ¼ cup (50 g) sugar and 2 teaspoons lemon zest; set aside.

17. In a separate bowl, stir together 3 Tablespoons (45 ml) melted butter and lemon juice; set aside.

18. While muffins are still hot, roll tops in melted butter mixture, then in sugar and lemon zest mixture. Place muffins on wire rack to cool.

Nutritional Information

Amount Per Serving: *Calories 230, Total Fat 9g, Saturated Fat 6g, Cholesterol 40mg, Sodium 135mg, Total Carbohydrate 34g, Dietary Fiber 1g, Sugars 15g, Protein 3g*

Apricot Breakfast Bread

Preparation: 15 minutes | ***Processing:*** 15–25 seconds
Bake Time: 45–60 minutes | ***Yield:*** 1 loaf (10 slices)

1 cup (120 g) whole wheat flour

1 cup (125 g) all-purpose flour

¼ teaspoon baking soda

2 teaspoons baking powder

¼ teaspoon salt

¼ cup (60 ml) water

1 orange, peeled, halved, and seeded

1 large egg

¾ cup (150 g) granulated sugar

2 Tablespoons (30 g) butter

1 cup (130 g) chopped dried apricots

½ cup (60 g) chopped pecans

1. Preheat oven to 350°F (180°C). Spray an 8½-inch x 4½-inch (21-cm x 11-cm) loaf pan with cooking spray.

2. Combine whole wheat flour, all-purpose flour, baking soda, baking powder, and salt in a medium-size mixing bowl. Set aside.

3. Place water, orange, egg, sugar, and butter into the Vitamix container in the order listed and firmly secure the lid.

4. Select Variable 1.

5. Start machine and slowly increase speed to Variable 6. Blend for 15 to 25 seconds. Stop machine.

6. Pour wet mixture into dry ingredients and stir gently by hand to combine. Fold in apricots and pecans.

7. Pour batter into prepared loaf pan. Bake for 45 to 60 minutes or until a knife inserted into the center comes out clean.

Nutritional Information

Amount Per Serving: *Calories 250, Total Fat 7g, Saturated Fat 2g, Cholesterol 5mg, Sodium 200mg, Total Carbohydrate 45g, Dietary Fiber 4g, Sugars 21g, Protein 4g*

Peanut Butter and Banana Muffins

Preparation: 20 minutes | **Processing:** 15 seconds
Bake Time: 20 minutes | **Yield:** 24 muffins

3 cups (375 g) all-purpose flour

1 Tablespoon baking powder

¼ teaspoon salt

¾ cup (180 ml) 2% milk

2 large eggs

1 Tablespoon vanilla extract

2 ripe medium bananas, peeled

¾ cup (190 g) peanut butter

⅓ cup (75 g) unsalted
butter, softened

1½ cups (300 g) granulated sugar

⅓ cup (25 g) uncooked rolled oats

1. Preheat oven to 400°F (200°C). Line two 12-muffin tins with cupcake papers.

2. Place flour, baking powder, and salt in a large-size mixing bowl and stir by hand to combine.

3. Place milk, eggs, vanilla, bananas, peanut butter, butter, and sugar into the Vitamix container in the order listed and firmly secure the lid.

4. Select Variable 5.

5. Start machine and blend for 15 seconds.

6. Pour wet mixture into dry ingredients and stir by hand to combine.

7. Spoon into lined muffin cups. Sprinkle oats over batter. Bake for 20 minutes or until a toothpick inserted into the center comes out clean. Cool on wire racks.

Nutritional Information

Amount Per Muffin: Calories 150, Total Fat 2.5g, Saturated Fat 0.5g, Cholesterol 15mg, Sodium 110mg, Total Carbohydrate 29g, Dietary Fiber 1g, Sugars 15g, Protein 4g

Peanut Butter Chocolate Chip Scones

Preparation: 15 minutes | **Processing:** 12 seconds plus Pulsing
Bake Time: 15–18 minutes | **Yield:** 8 scones

2 cups (250 g) all-purpose flour

¼ cup (50 g) granulated sugar

2 teaspoons baking powder

¼ teaspoon baking soda

¼ teaspoon salt

¼ cup (60 g) cold butter,
cut in 8 pats

½ cup (120 g) miniature
chocolate chips

⅔ cup (160 ml) milk

1 large egg

½ cup (120 g) peanut butter

1. Preheat oven to 375°F (190°C). Line a cookie sheet with parchment paper.

2. Place flour, sugar, baking powder, soda, and salt into the Vitamix container and firmly secure the lid.

3. Select Variable 4.

4. Start machine and blend for 2 seconds. Stop machine and remove lid.

5. Add butter to the Vitamix container and firmly secure the lid.

6. Select Variable 4.

7. Pulse 6 times. Pour mixture into a large bowl. Stir in chocolate chips.

8. Add milk, egg, and peanut butter to the Vitamix container and firmly secure the lid.

9. Select Variable 2.

10. Start machine and blend for 10 seconds. Pour over dry ingredients. Stir just until moistened.

11. Flour a work surface. Scoop mixture onto floured surface and knead 5 or 6 times. Form into 1 disk, 8 inches (20 cm) in diameter. Cut into 8 wedges. Place wedges 2 inches (5 cm) apart on cookie sheet.

12. Bake for 15 to 18 minutes or until golden brown and set. Do not over bake. Store at room temperature in an airtight container.

Nutritional Information

Amount Per Serving: *Calories 380, Total Fat 19g, Saturated Fat 8g, Cholesterol 40mg, Sodium 330mg, Total Carbohydrate 44g, Dietary Fiber 3g, Sugars 17g, Protein 10g*

Cranberry Nut Bread

Preparation: 15 minutes | **Processing:** 15 seconds
Bake Time: 60 minutes | **Yield:** 1 loaf (10 slices)

1½ teaspoons baking powder

½ teaspoon baking soda

1 teaspoon salt

1 cup (120 g) whole wheat flour

1 cup (125 g) all-purpose flour

1 orange, peeled, halved, and seeded

2-inch (5 cm) strip of orange peel

¼ cup (60 ml) light olive oil or vegetable oil

¾ cup (180 ml) milk

1 cup (200 g) granulated sugar

1 large egg

1 cup (100 g) fresh cranberries

½ cup (60 g) chopped walnuts

1. Preheat oven to 350°F (180°C). Spray an 8½-inch x 4½-inch (21-cm x 11-cm) loaf pan with cooking spray.

2. Combine baking powder, baking soda, salt, whole wheat flour, and all-purpose flour in a large-size mixing bowl. Set aside.

3. Place orange, orange peel, oil, milk, sugar, and egg into the Vitamix container in the order listed and firmly secure the lid.

4. Select Variable 1.

5. Start machine and slowly increase speed to Variable 8.

6. Blend for 15 seconds.

7. Pour wet mixture into dry ingredients and stir by hand just until combined.

8. Gently fold in cranberries and walnuts.

9. Spread the batter in the prepared loaf pan.

10. Bake for 60 minutes or until a knife inserted into the center comes out clean.

Nutritional Information

Amount Per Serving: *Calories 280, Total Fat 10g, Saturated Fat 1.5g, Cholesterol 20mg, Sodium 380mg, Total Carbohydrate 43g, Dietary Fiber 3g, Sugars 23g, Protein 5g*

Rosemary Focaccia

Preparation: 10 minutes | **Processing:** 15 seconds plus Pulsing
Bake Time: 18–25 minutes | **Yield:** 8 servings

1 cup (240 ml) warm water,
105–115°F (40–45°C)

1 Tablespoon honey

1 package (¼ ounce)
rapid rising yeast

2 Tablespoons (30 ml)
light olive oil, divided use

2 cups (250 g) all-purpose flour

½ cup (60 g) whole wheat flour

1 teaspoon coarse salt

2 Tablespoons (5 g) fresh
rosemary, divided use

2 Tablespoons (10 g) grated
Parmesan cheese

1. Preheat oven to 400°F (200°C). Line a baking sheet with silpat mat or parchment paper. Combine water and honey in a small bowl. Sprinkle yeast over warm water and let stand 5 minutes. Stir in 1 Tablespoon olive oil.

2. Place flours, salt, and 1 Tablespoon rosemary into the Vitamix container and firmly secure the lid.

3. Select Variable 1. Start machine and blend until a hole forms in the center, about 5 seconds. Remove lid plug. Add yeast mixture through the lid plug opening and slowly increase speed to Variable 3. Mix until dough forms, about 10 seconds.

4. Stop machine and scrape the sides of the container with a rubber spatula, pulling dough to the center.

5. Select Variable 3.

6. Pulse 10 times. Scrape the sides of the container and repeat scraping and pulsing 4 times until dough is elastic.

7. Allow dough to drop onto lightly floured surface and shape into a ball. (Use a rubber spatula to remove any remaining dough.) Cover loosely and let stand 10 minutes.

8. Press dough onto prepared baking sheet to ½-inch (1½-cm) thickness. Lightly cover dough with a clean towel and let rise 15 to 20 minutes. Use the bottom of a wooden spoon or your knuckles to press indentations into the dough. Drizzle with the remaining olive oil, rosemary, and Parmesan cheese. Sprinkle with salt, if desired.

9. Bake for 18 to 25 minutes or until edges are browned.

Nutritional Information

Amount Per Serving: *Calories 190, Total Fat 4.5g, Saturated Fat 1g, Cholesterol 0mg, Sodium 260mg, Total Carbohydrate 32g, Dietary Fiber 2g, Sugars 2g, Protein 5g*

Bacon Cheddar Cornbread

Preparation: 15 minutes | **Processing:** 15 seconds plus Pulsing
Bake Time: 23–28 minutes | **Yield:** 9 servings

1 cup (125 g) all-purpose flour

1 cup (150 g) cornmeal

2 teaspoons baking powder

½ teaspoon baking soda

¼ teaspoon coarse salt

1 cup (240 ml) buttermilk

¼ cup (50 g) granulated sugar

2 large eggs

3 Tablespoons (45 ml) canola oil

4 ounces (115 g) Cheddar cheese, cubed

3 slices bacon, cooked and crumbled

1. Preheat oven to 375°F (190°C). Spray an 8-inch x 8-inch (20-cm x 20-cm) baking pan with nonstick cooking spray.

2. Combine flour, cornmeal, baking powder, baking soda, and salt in a medium-size mixing bowl. Set aside.

3. Place buttermilk, sugar, eggs, and oil into the Vitamix container in the order listed and firmly secure the lid.

4. Select Variable 1.

5. Start machine and slowly increase speed to Variable 4.

6. Blend for 10 seconds until smooth. Stop machine and remove lid.

7. Add cheese to the Vitamix container and firmly secure the lid.

8. Select Variable 3. Pulse 8 to 10 times until cheese is chopped. Remove lid.

9. Add flour mixture to the Vitamix container and firmly secure the lid.

10. Start machine and blend for 5 seconds until smooth. Remove lid plug.

11. Add bacon through the lid plug opening and replace lid plug.

12. Pulse 5 to 6 times to incorporate. Pour batter into prepared pan. Bake for 23 to 28 minutes until lightly browned.

Nutritional Information

Amount Per Serving: *Calories 260, Total Fat 12g, Saturated Fat 4g, Cholesterol 60mg, Sodium 410mg, Total Carbohydrate 29g, Dietary Fiber 1g, Sugars 7g, Protein 9g*

Whole Wheat Crêpes

Preparation: 45 minutes | **Processing:** 15 seconds
Cook Time: 10 minutes | **Yield:** 14 crêpes

1 cup (120 g) whole wheat flour	6 large eggs
1 cup (125 g) all-purpose flour	4 teaspoons canola oil
½ teaspoon salt	2 teaspoons granulated sugar
1 cup (240 ml) 2% milk	1 cup (240 ml) seltzer water

1. Place whole wheat flour, all-purposed flour, and salt in a medium-size mixing bowl and stir by hand to combine.

2. Place milk, eggs, oil, and sugar into the Vitamix container in the order listed and firmly secure the lid.

3. Select Variable 1.

4. Start machine and slowly increase speed to Variable 5.

5. Blend for 15 seconds.

6. Pour wet mixture into dry ingredients whisk to combine. Cover and refrigerate at least 30 minutes.

7. Slowly whisk seltzer water into the batter.

8. Spray a nonstick skillet with cooking spray and place over medium-high heat. Ladle ⅓ cup (80 ml) batter onto the center of the pan and immediately tilt and rotate the pan to spread the batter evenly across the skillet.

9. Cook about 30 seconds, until underside is lightly browned. Use a heat-resistant spatula to lift the edge of the crêpe and then grab with your fingers to flip. Cook until second side is lightly browned. Slide onto plate. Repeat with remaining batter.

Nutritional Information

Amount Per Crêpe: *Calories 120, Total Fat 4g, Saturated Fat 1g, Cholesterol 80mg, Sodium 120mg, Total Carbohydrate 15g, Dietary Fiber 1g, Sugars 2g, Protein 5g*

Coconut Waffles

Preparation: 20 minutes | ***Processing:*** 10 seconds | ***Yield:*** 7 waffles

1¾ cups (220 g)
all-purpose flour

2 Tablespoons (25 g)
granulated sugar

1 Tablespoon baking powder

3 large eggs

1 (14-ounce / 400-ml)
can light coconut milk

6 Tablespoons (85 g)
butter, softened

¾ cup (60 g) unsweetened
shredded coconut

½ cup (70 g) almonds,
chopped and toasted

1. Place flour, sugar, and baking powder in a medium-size mixing bowl and stir by hand to combine.

2. Place eggs, coconut milk, butter, and coconut into the Vitamix container in the order listed and firmly secure the lid.

3. Select Variable 5.

4. Start machine and blend for 10 seconds.

5. Pour wet mixture into dry ingredients and stir by hand to combine.

6. Place ½ cup (120 ml) batter onto a preheated waffle maker. Bake according to manufacturer's instructions.

7. Garnish with toasted almonds.

Nutritional Information

Amount Per Waffle: *Calories 390, Total Fat 26g, Saturated Fat 15g, Cholesterol 105mg, Sodium 340mg, Total Carbohydrate 33g, Dietary Fiber 3g, Sugars 5g, Protein 9g*

Oatmeal Cranberry Pancakes

Preparation: 15 minutes | **Processing:** 20 seconds
Yield: 3 cups (600 ml) or 10 pancakes

1½ cups (360 ml) milk

1 large egg

1 cup (120 g) whole wheat flour

2 teaspoons baking powder

½ teaspoon baking soda

½ teaspoon salt

¼ cup (40 g) flaxseed meal

¾ cup (115 g) uncooked
rolled oats

¼ cup (30 g) dried cranberries

2 Tablespoons (20 g)
unsalted sunflower seeds

1. Place milk, egg, flour, baking powder, baking soda, salt, and flaxseed meal into the Vitamix container in the order listed and firmly secure the lid.

2. Select Variable 1.

3. Start machine and slowly increase speed to Variable 8.

4. Blend for 10 seconds. Stop machine and remove lid. Add oats, cranberries, and sunflower seeds into the Vitamix container and firmly secure the lid.

5. Select Variable 1.

6. Start machine and blend for 10 seconds, using the tamper if necessary to press the ingredients into the blades.

7. Let batter sit for 5 to 10 minutes before cooking to yield best texture and flavor.

Nutritional Information

Amount Per Serving: *Calories 120, Total Fat 4g, Saturated Fat 1g, Cholesterol 20mg, Sodium 180mg, Total Carbohydrate 18g, Dietary Fiber 3g, Sugars 4g, Protein 5g*

Desserts

Now it's easier than ever *to create enticing, guilt-free desserts. In addition to fresh fruit sorbets, enjoy delectable treats such as Dark Chocloate Mousse and Vegan Raisin Almond Cookies.*

Desserts

FROZEN DESSERTS / BAKED DESSERTS / DESSERT CONDIMENTS

Basic Vanilla Milkshake

Preparation: 5 minutes | **Processing:** 15 seconds | **Yield:** 4¾ cups (1.1 l)

4 cups (520 g) vanilla ice cream

1¾ cups (420 ml) milk

2½ teaspoons vanilla extract

1. Place all ingredients into the Vitamix container in the order listed and firmly secure the lid.

2. Select Variable 1.

3. Start machine and slowly increase speed to Variable 8.

4. Blend for 15 seconds, or until desired consistency is reached.

Nutritional Information

Amount Per 1 Cup (240 ml) Serving: *Calories 290, Total Fat 15g, Saturated Fat 8g, Cholesterol 45mg, Sodium 95mg, Total Carbohydrate 30g, Dietary Fiber 0g, Sugars 28g, Protein 8g*

Bright Idea

Family Milkshakes

Let every member of the family create a customised milkshake. Offer any of the following ingredients and add them to the Vanilla Milkshake recipe in Step 1 for a tasty new family tradition.

¼ cup (45 g)
chocolate milk powder

½ cup (60 g)
fresh raspberries

½ cup (75 g)
fresh blueberries

4 medium strawberries

2 chocolate sandwich cookies

1 Tablespoon jam

1 Tablespoon chocolate hazelnut spread

1 teaspoon honey

2 Tablespoons (15 g)
crunch cereal or granola

2 Tablespoons (30 ml)
maple syrup

Peanut Butter Cup Milkshake

Preparation: 5 minutes | **Processing:** 30 seconds | **Yield:** 3 cups (720 ml)

¼ cup plus 2 Tablespoons (90 ml) milk

3 cups (400 g) vanilla ice cream

3 Tablespoons (45 g) peanut butter

3 Tablespoons (45 ml) chocolate syrup

1. Place all ingredients into the Vitamix container in the order listed and firmly secure the lid.

2. Select Variable 1.

3. Start machine and slowly increase speed to Variable 8.

4. Blend for 30 seconds, or until desired consistency is reached.

Nutritional Information

Amount Per 1 Cup (240 ml) Serving: *Calories 460, Total Fat 27g, Saturated Fat 11g, Cholesterol 50mg, Sodium 150mg, Total Carbohydrate 46g, Dietary Fiber 2g, Sugars 40g, Protein 11g*

Chocolate Covered Strawberry Milkshake

Preparation: 5 minutes | ***Processing:*** 15 seconds | ***Yield:*** 3½ cups (840 ml)

3 cups (400 g) vanilla ice cream

¼ cup plus 2 Tablespoons (90 ml) milk

1½ teaspoons vanilla extract

6 fresh strawberries, hulled

3 Tablespoons (45 g) chocolate milk powder

1. Place all ingredients into the Vitamix container in the order listed and firmly secure the lid.

2. Select Variable 1.

3. Start machine and slowly increase speed to Variable 8.

4. Blend for 15 seconds, using the tamper to press the ingredients into the blades.

Nutritional Information

Amount Per 1 Cup (240 ml) Serving: *Calories 340, Total Fat 17g, Saturated Fat 9g, Cholesterol 45mg, Sodium 105mg, Total Carbohydrate 42g, Dietary Fiber 1g, Sugars 38g, Protein 7g*

Strawberry Yogurt Freeze ❄

Preparation: 10 minutes | *Processing:* 55 seconds | *Yield:* 5 cups (1.2 l)

1½ cups (360 g) vanilla yogurt

1½ pounds (680 g) frozen unsweetened strawberries

1. Place all ingredients into the Vitamix container in the order listed and firmly secure the lid.

2. Select Variable 1 or the Frozen Dessert program.

3. Start machine, slowly increase to its highest speed, and blend for 55 seconds; or start machine and allow programmed cycle to complete.

4. Serve immediately.

Nutritional Information

Amount Per ½ Cup (120 ml) Serving: *Calories 50, Total Fat 0g, Saturated Fat 0g, Cholesterol 0mg, Sodium 25mg, Total Carbohydrate 11g, Dietary Fiber 1g, Sugars 8g, Protein 2g*

Berry Sorbet with Mixed Spices ❄

Preparation: 25 minutes | **Processing:** 1 minute 15 seconds
Yield: 4½ cups (1.1 l)

½ ounce (15 g) fresh ginger
root, peeled

1 cup (240 ml) cold water

½ cup (100 g) granulated sugar

1 cup (150 g) frozen unsweetened
strawberries, thawed for 20 minutes

1 cup (140 g) frozen unsweetened
blueberries, thawed for 20 minutes

1 cup (140 g) frozen unsweetened
blackberries, thawed for 20 minutes

1 cup (140 g) frozen unsweetened
raspberries, thawed for 20 minutes

2 cups (300 g) frozen pitted Bing
cherries, thawed for 20 minutes

½ cup (13 g) fresh mint leaves

⅛ teaspoon ground cloves

⅛ teaspoon ground allspice

¼ teaspoon ground nutmeg

½ teaspoon ground cinnamon

1 teaspoon vanilla extract

1. Place ginger, water, and sugar into the Vitamix container and firmly secure lid.

2. Select Variable 1.

3. Start machine and slowly increase speed to Variable 8. Blend for 20 seconds until ginger is finely chopped. Stop machine and remove lid. Add berries, mint, cloves, allspice, nutmeg, cinnamon, and vanilla to the container and firmly secure lid.

4. Select Variable 1 or the Frozen Dessert program.

5. Start machine, slowly increase to its highest speed, and blend for 55 seconds, using the tamper to press the ingredients into the blades; or start machine and allow programmed cycle to complete, using the tamper to press the ingredients into the blades.

6. Serve immediately.

Nutritional Information

Amount Per ½ Cup (120 ml) Serving: *Calories 90, Total Fat 0g, Saturated Fat 0g, Cholesterol 0mg, Sodium 0mg, Total Carbohydrate 24g, Dietary Fiber 3g, Sugars 19g, Protein 1g*

Mixed Fruit and Chocolate Freeze

Preparation: 10 minutes | **Processing:** 55 seconds | **Yield:** 4 cups (960 ml) (8 servings)

1½ cups (360 ml) low-fat vanilla or plain yogurt

1 cup (145 g) coarsely chopped dark chocolate

1½ teaspoons vanilla extract

1½ pounds (680 g) frozen unsweetened fruit, half strawberries
and half mango chunks, softened for 5 minutes

1. Place all ingredients into the Vitamix container in the order listed and
firmly secure the lid.

2. Select Variable 1 or the Frozen Dessert program.

3. Start machine, slowly increase to its highest speed, and blend for 55 seconds, using the
tamper to press the ingredients into the blades; or start machine and allow programmed
cycle to complete, using the tamper to press the ingredients into the blades.

4. Serve immediately.

Nutritional Information

Amount Per Serving: *Calories 190, Total Fat 8g, Saturated Fat 5g, Cholesterol 5mg,
Sodium 35mg, Total Carbohydrate 26g, Dietary Fiber 4g, Sugars 19g, Protein 4g*

Cookies and Cream Freeze

Preparation: 10 minutes | **Processing:** Pulsing | **Yield:** 2 cups (480 ml) (4 servings)

2½ cups (340 g) vanilla ice cream

1 ounce (30 ml) chocolate syrup

6 chocolate sandwich cookies, divided use

1 ounce (30 g) white chocolate

1. Place ice cream, syrup, 4 cookies, and white chocolate into the Vitamix container in the order listed and firmly secure the lid.

2. Select Variable 8.

3. Pulse 18 to 20 times, using the tamper to press the ingredients into the blades.

4. Add remaining cookies and Pulse 6 times to incorporate.

Nutritional Information

Amount Per ½ Cup (120 ml) Serving: Calories 320, Total Fat 17g, Saturated Fat 8g, Cholesterol 35mg, Sodium 140mg, Total Carbohydrate 39g, Dietary Fiber 1g, Sugars 32g, Protein 5g

Herbed Apple Granita

Preparation: 10 minutes plus overnight freezing | **Processing:** 40 seconds – 1 minute
Yield: 4 cups (960 ml) (8 servings)

3 cups (720 ml) apple juice

4 teaspoons fresh lemon juice

½ cup (120 ml) honey

½ cup (50 g) fresh tarragon leaves

1. Place all ingredients into the Vitamix container in the order listed and firmly secure the lid.

2. Select Variable 1.

3. Start machine and slowly increase to its highest speed.

4. Blend for 20 to 30 seconds.

5. Pour into two standard ice cube trays and freeze overnight. Let trays thaw at room temperature for 10 minutes.

6. Place ice cubes into the Vitamix container and firmly secure the lid.

7. Select Variable 1.

8. Start machine and slowly increase speed to its highest speed.

9. Blend for 20 to 30 seconds, using the tamper to press the ice cubes into the blades. The sound of the motor will change and the mixture will start to flow freely through the blades. Toward the end of processing, leave the tamper inserted through the lid plug opening to encourage the formation of four mounds.

Nutritional Information

Amount Per Serving: *Calories 110, Total Fat 0g, Saturated Fat 0g, Cholesterol 0mg, Sodium 10mg, Total Carbohydrate 28g, Dietary Fiber 0g, Sugars 26g, Protein 0g*

Vegan Raisin Almond Cookies

Preparation: 20 minutes | ***Processing:*** 30 seconds
Bake Time: 14 minutes | ***Yield:*** 44 cookies

¾ cup (180 ml) cold, strong coffee

¼ cup (55 g) vegan margarine, melted and cooled

1 teaspoon almond extract

½ cup (80 g) pitted prunes

1⅓ cups (265 g) granulated sugar

1 Tablespoon flaxseed

2¼ cups (280 g) all-purpose flour

¾ teaspoon baking powder

¾ teaspoon baking soda

¼ teaspoon salt

¾ cup (120 g) golden raisins

½ cup (70 g) chopped almonds

1. Preheat oven to 375°F (190°C). Line a baking sheet with silpat or parchment paper.

2. Place coffee, margarine, almond extract, prunes, sugar, and flaxseed into the Vitamix container in the order listed and firmly secure the lid. Select Variable 1.

3. Start machine and slowly increase to its highest speed.

4. Blend for 30 seconds.

5. Place flour, baking powder, baking soda, and salt into a medium-size mixing bowl. Stir by hand to combine.

6. Pour wet mixture into dry ingredients and stir by hand to combine. Stir in raisins and almonds.

7. Drop by rounded Tablespoons onto prepared baking sheet.

8. Bake for 14 minutes. Transfer to a wire rack to cool.

Nutritional Information

Amount Per Cookie: *Calories 80, Total Fat 2g, Saturated Fat 0g, Cholesterol 0mg, Sodium 65mg, Total Carbohydrate 15g, Dietary Fiber 1g, Sugars 9g, Protein 1g*

Lemon Curd ♨

Preparation: 10 minutes | **Processing:** 6 minutes 15 seconds
Yield: 3½ cups (840 ml)

5 large eggs

½ cup (120 ml) fresh lemon juice

Zest of 3 lemons

1½ cups (300 g) granulated sugar

⅛ teaspoon salt

½ cup (120 g) unsalted butter, room temperature, cut into small pieces

1. Place eggs, lemon juice, lemon zest, sugar, and salt into the Vitamix container and firmly secure the lid.

2. Select Variable 1 or the Hot Soup program.

3. Start machine, slowly increase to its highest speed, and blend for 5 minutes 45 seconds; or start machine and allow programmed cycle to complete.

4. Select Variable 1.

5. Start machine and slowly increase speed to Variable 3. Remove the lid plug. Add butter through the lid plug opening and secure lid plug.

6. Blend an additional 30 seconds.

Nutritional Information

Amount Per ¼ Cup (60 ml) Serving: *Calories 170, Total Fat 9g, Saturated Fat 5g, Cholesterol 90mg, Sodium 50mg, Total Carbohydrate 22g, Dietary Fiber 0g, Sugars 22g, Protein 3g*

Low-Fat Pumpkin Pie

Preparation: 15 minutes | **Processing:** 10–15 seconds
Bake Time: 55 minutes | **Yield:** 3 pies (24 slices)

1 cup (240 ml) egg substitute

3½ cups (850 g) canned pumpkin

1½ cups (300 g) granulated sugar

1 teaspoon salt

2 teaspoons ground cinnamon

1 teaspoon ground ginger

½ teaspoon ground cloves

3 cups (720 ml) evaporated
nonfat milk

3 unbaked 9-inch (23-cm)
deep dish pie shells

Whipped Cream
(See recipe in Kitchen Basics)

1. Preheat oven to 425°F (220°C).

2. Place egg substitute, pumpkin, sugar, salt, cinnamon, ginger, cloves, and evaporated milk into the Vitamix container in the order listed and firmly secure the lid.

3. Select Variable 1.

4. Start machine and slowly increase speed to Variable 5.

5. Blend for 10 to 15 seconds.

6. Pour into pie shells.

7. Bake for 15 minutes. Reduce oven temperature to 350°F (180°C). Bake for 40 minutes. Pie is done when a knife inserted into the center comes out clean. Filling will be soft, but firms up as it sets and cools.

8. Chill and serve with whipped cream.

Nutritional Information

Amount Per Slice: *Calories 220, Total Fat 8g, Saturated Fat 2.5g, Cholesterol 0mg, Sodium 250mg, Total Carbohydrate 32g, Dietary Fiber 2g, Sugars 17g, Protein 5g*

Chocolate Sour Cream Cupcakes

Preparation: 15 minutes | **Processing:** 20 seconds
Bake Time: 20–25 minutes | **Yield:** 18 cupcakes

4 ounces (115 g) unsweetened chocolate, chopped

1 cup (240 ml) hot, strong brewed coffee

2 cups (250 g) all-purpose flour

¾ teaspoon baking soda

½ teaspoon salt

2 cups (400 g) granulated sugar

½ cup (120 ml) canola oil

2 large eggs

½ cup (120 g) sour cream

1. Preheat oven to 375°F (190°C). Line muffin pan with cupcake papers.

2. In a medium saucepan, combine chocolate and hot coffee over low heat. Stir continuously until chocolate has melted.

3. Combine flour, baking soda, and salt in a medium-size mixing bowl and set aside.

4. Place sugar, oil, eggs, and sour cream into the Vitamix container in the order listed and firmly secure the lid.

5. Select Variable 1.

6. Start machine and slowly increase speed to Variable 5. Blend for 20 seconds.

7. Transfer blended mixture and melted chocolate into dry ingredients and stir by hand until combined.

8. Fill muffin cups two-thirds full. Bake for 20 to 25 minutes.

Nutritional Information

Amount Per Serving: *Calories 250, Total Fat 11g, Saturated Fat 3.5g, Cholesterol 25mg, Sodium 130mg, Total Carbohydrate 35g, Dietary Fiber 1g, Sugars 23g, Protein 3g*

Brown Sugar Surprise Cupcakes

Preparation: 20 minutes | **Processing:** 30 seconds
Bake Time: 20–25 minutes | **Yield:** 24 full-size cupcakes

1¼ cups (300 ml) milk

2 large eggs

1½ teaspoons vanilla extract

⅔ cup (150 g) unsalted butter, softened

1¾ cups (350 g) granulated sugar

2½ cups (310 g) all-purpose flour

2½ teaspoons baking powder

½ teaspoon salt

½ cup (110 g) firmly packed brown sugar

¼ cup (25 g) finely chopped pecans

1 teaspoon ground cinnamon

1. Preheat oven to 350°F (180°C). Line a 24 muffin tin with paper cups.

2. Place milk, eggs, vanilla, butter, and sugar into the Vitamix container in the order listed and firmly secure the lid.

3. Select Variable 1.

4. Start machine and slowly increase speed to Variable 7. Blend for 30 seconds.

5. In a large-size mixing bowl, combine flour, baking powder, and salt.

6. Pour wet mixture into dry ingredients and stir by hand to combine.

7. In a small bowl, whisk together brown sugar, pecans, and cinnamon.

8. Spoon 1 Tablespoon of batter into each prepared muffin cup. Sprinkle 1 teaspoon of the brown sugar mixture on top of the batter. Repeat layers by spooning remaining batter evenly between cups, and sprinkle remaining brown sugar mixture on top.

9. Bake for 20 to 25 minutes, or until a toothpick inserted into the center comes out clean. Cool on wire racks for 10 minutes. Remove cupcakes from muffin cups and cool completely.

Nutritional Information

Amount Per Cupcake: *Calories 190, Total Fat 7g, Saturated Fat 3.5g, Cholesterol 30mg, Sodium 115mg, Total Carbohydrate 30g, Dietary Fiber 1g, Sugars 20g, Protein 2g*

Dark Chocolate Mousse

Preparation: 10 minutes | **Processing:** 20–25 seconds | **Yield:** 3 cups (720 ml)

5 ounces (140 g) bittersweet chocolate, finely chopped

2 Tablespoons (30 g) unsalted butter, diced

2 Tablespoons (30 ml) hot coffee

1½ cups (360 ml) heavy cream

2 Tablespoons (15 g) powdered sugar

1. Combine chocolate, butter, and coffee in the top of a double boiler over hot, but not simmering water, stirring frequently until smooth. Remove from heat and let cool completely.

2. When chocolate mixture is cold, place cream and sugar into the Vitamix container in the order listed and firmly secure the lid.

3. Select Variable 1.

4. Start machine and slowly increase speed to Variable 8.

5. Blend for 20 to 25 seconds, or until firmly whipped.

6. Scrape mixture into the bowl atop cooled chocolate; fold in cream just until incorporated and serve immediately.

Nutritional Information

Amount Per ½ Cup (120 ml) Serving: *Calories 370, Total Fat 36g, Saturated Fat 22g, Cholesterol 90mg, Sodium 25mg, Total Carbohydrate 15g, Dietary Fiber 3g, Sugars 9g, Protein 4g*

Vanilla Custard Sauce

Preparation: 10 minutes | **Processing:** 5 minutes 45 seconds | **Yield:** 4½ cups (1.0 l)

6 egg yolks

1½ cups (360 ml) half & half

¼ cup (30 g) all-purpose flour

½ cup (100 g) granulated sugar

⅛ teaspoon salt

1 Tablespoon vanilla extract

1 Tablespoon butter

1. Place all ingredients into the Vitamix container in the order listed and firmly secure the lid.

2. Select Variable 1 or the Hot Soup program.

3. Start machine, slowly increase to its highest speed, and blend for 5 minutes 45 seconds; or start machine and allow programmed cycle to complete.

Nutritional Information

Amount Per ¼ Cup (60 ml) Serving: *Calories 80, Total Fat 4.5g, Saturated Fat 2.5g, Cholesterol 70mg, Sodium 35mg, Total Carbohydrate 8g, Dietary Fiber 0g, Sugars 6g, Protein 2g*

Mixed Berry Purée ♨

Preparation: 10 minutes | **Processing:** 5 minutes 45 seconds | **Yield:** 3½ cups (840 ml)

½ cup (120 ml) water

1 Tablespoon fresh lemon juice

1½ cups (210 g) frozen unsweetened raspberries, partially thawed

1½ cups (150 g) frozen unsweetened strawberries, partially thawed

1 cup (155 g) frozen unsweetened blueberries, partially thawed

¾ cup (150 g) granulated sugar

1. Place all ingredients into the Vitamix container in the order listed and firmly secure the lid.

2. Select Variable 1 or the Hot Soup program.

3. Start machine, slowly increase to its highest speed, and blend for 5 minutes 45 seconds; or start machine and allow programmed cycle to complete.

Nutritional Information

Amount Per ¼ Cup (60 ml) Serving: *Calories 60, Total Fat 0g, Saturated Fat 0g, Cholesterol 0mg, Sodium 0mg, Total Carbohydrate 15g, Dietary Fiber 1g, Sugars 13g, Protein 0g*